BLACK WRITERS
IN NEW ENGLAND

African Meeting House, Smith Court, Boston, Mass., *circa* 1890, where Frederick Douglass, Charles Lenox Remond, and other black abolitionists lectured.

(Society for the Preservation of New England Antiquities)

BLACK WRITERS
IN NEW ENGLAND

A Bibliography, with Biographical Notes,
of Books By and About Afro-American Writers
Associated with New England in the
Collection of Afro-American Literature

*Suffolk University   Museum of Afro-American History
Boston African American National Historic Site*

Edward Clark

*810.3
C L A*

National Park Service   Boston   1985

U.S. Department of the Interior
National Park Service
Boston African American National Historic Site
15 State Street
Boston, Massachusetts 02109

Printed in the United States of America
First Edition

Library of Congress Cataloging in Publication Data
Clark, Edward, 1923–
    Black writers in New England.
    1. American literature—Afro-American authors—
Bio-bibliography. 2. American literature—New
England—Bio-bibliography. 3. Afro-American authors—
New England—Biography—Dictionaries. 4. Museum of
Afro-American History (Boston, Mass.) I. Title.
Z1229.N39C57   1985 [PS153.N5]   016.81′09′896   85-10568
ISBN 0-934441-01-4

30772

Cover photograph: Dorothy West signing her novel *The Living Is Easy* in 1948.
(Courtesy William Bowles)

To Leah

CONTENTS

PREFACE

This bibliography is a culmination and a new beginning.

It is the culmination of fourteen years of work by Edward Clark creating, developing, and publicizing the Collection of Afro-American Literature.

Edward Clark is eminently fitted for this vital service. Clark wrote his doctoral dissertation on race in James Fenimore Cooper's novels. He joined the faculty of Suffolk University in 1961 and in 1969 taught his first course in black literature. It was in preparation for this course that Clark began ordering books in black American literature for the University Library.

In 1971, Clark approached J. Marcus Mitchell at the Museum of Afro-American History with an idea that developed into the Collection of Afro-American Literature, a joint project of Suffolk University and the Museum of Afro-American History. From the very beginning, Clark and I believed that the Collection, though national in scope, should give a special emphasis to Afro-American writers associated with New England. I had no doubt that this would mean a significant number of authors. Why not? Africans have been settled in New England from at least 1638 and possibly from before. In the slavery period Afro-Americans were writing. In the antebellum 19th century the major free black communities in the North were in Pennsylvania and New England. New England colleges have attracted black students since the first Afro-Americans attended Bowdoin in Maine, Amherst in Massachusetts, and Middlebury in Vermont—all in the 1820's. Yet, I was not prepared for the number of black writers Clark has identified as associated with this region. Clark brings a persistence and catholic approach to this work that has produced a bibliography that will point out new directions for scholars for years to come.

In composition, as in organization and content, this bibliography will not be found wanting. The brief biographical sketches should be the seeds for the germination of countless papers. Librarians and collectors have a checklist here that can be used in many ways. The list of authors with no holdings in the Collection is a challenge to Clark's successor. The publication itself of this bibliography will begin the process of compiling a supplement to it.

This work marks a new beginning for the Collection of Afro-American Literature. It is most appropriate that Clark completes this work as he prepares to take early retirement from his Suffolk professorship. He leaves a work that will transform the role of the Collection of Afro-American Literature into a major regional Afro-American collection of national importance. He has set a standard for Afro-American regional bibliographies and this work is "a call" that similar bibliographies be produced throughout the country.

Thank you, Edward Clark.

Byron Rushing
State House, Boston
May 10, 1985

ACKNOWLEDGMENTS

My thanks are due a number of people who helped make the book possible. Byron Rushing, president of the Museum of Afro-American History, lent strong support in this as in other projects of the Collection of Afro-American Literature. His enthusiasm and unwavering commitment to black culture, over many years of our working together, have been an inspiration to me. The staff of the Mildred F. Sawyer Library, Suffolk University, and the director, Edmund G. Hamann, met my frequent requests with cheerful efficiency that much facilitated my work. Without the following pioneer scholars in black literary biography, this book could not have been done: Ann Allen Schockley and Sue P. Chandler, *Living Black American Authors: A Biographical Dictionary* (1973); Leaonead Pack Bailey, *Broadside Authors and Artists: An Illustrated Biographical Directory* (1974); Theressa Gunnels Bush, Carol Fairbanks Myers, and Esther Spring Arata, *Black American Writers Past and Present: A Biographical and Bibliographical Dictionary* (1975); James A. Page, *Selected Black American Authors: An Illustrated Bio-Bibliography* (1977); and Rayford W. Logan and Michael R. Winston, *Dictionary of American Negro Biography* (1982). Professors Allan D. Austin, Springfield College, Mass., author of *African Muslims in Antebellum America: A Sourcebook* (1984); Joe Weixlmann, Indiana State University, editor of *Black American Literature Forum*; and Russell C. Brignano, Pennsylvania State University, replied generously to my solicitation of aid. Dr. Brignano's *Black Americans in Autobiography* (1984), a model of scholarship, was a fruitful source for identifying and describing writers.

Across New England are kind people working in offices of schools, colleges, universities, and medical and theological schools who gave immediate care to phone inquiries about past and present students and faculty. Writers themselves were uniformly cooperative in receiving unexpected phone calls; their responses often led me to other writers. Marilyn Richardson, historical essayist, was especially helpful. Two members of the National Park Service—John J. Burchill, superintendent, Boston National Historical Park, and Dorothea L. Powell, site manager, Boston African American National Historic Site—arranged crucial financial support. The warm-hearted expertise of K. Powell Associates, Graphic Design, Boston, made production of the book a true pleasure.

I thank these good people, one and all.

E.C.

Suffolk University
April 2, 1985

INTRODUCTION

Collection of Afro-American Literature

Since 1971 Suffolk University and the Museum of Afro-American History have been developing jointly a Collection of Afro-American Literature. In 1981 the newly established Boston African American National Historic Site, under auspices of the National Park Service, joined in cooperation with the project. The Collection aims to include poetry, drama, fiction, and non-fiction prose of all important black American writers from the eighteenth century to the present. It contains related historical, literary-historical, critical, biographical, and bibliographical works by writers of all races, as well as periodicals. Always growing, the Collection has 3500 titles and 3800 volumes. It is housed in the University's Mildred F. Sawyer Library.

The Collection is unique in Massachusetts in its focus on literature. In Boston it furnishes a resource in a central city location where members of the University, Museum, and metropolitan academic communities can find Afro-American literature and ancillary works.

Establishment of the Collection is a cooperative step by neighboring institutions on Beacon Hill to deepen our understanding of black American culture and foster closer racial relations. The University is located near the Massachusetts State House. The Museum occupies the African Meeting House nearby. The African Meeting House, built in 1806, is the oldest standing black church building in the United States. The Boston African American National Historic Site consists of sixteen buildings and monuments on Beacon Hill, including the Meeting House, that are important in nineteenth century black Boston history.

A list of acquisitions to the Collection is published annually in March. Inquiries about the list and the Collection are welcome.

Afro-American Writers Associated with New England

A special interest of the Collection is Afro-American writers associated with New England—with Maine, New Hampshire, Vermont, Massachusetts, Rhode Island, Connecticut. The association is based on a writer meeting one or more of the following criteria:
• Born in New England
• Studied there
• Lived there
• Worked there.
These criteria are applied in the present volume.

In Section I, "Books By and About Afro-American Writers Associated with New England in the Collection of Afro-American Literature," are listed writers that I have identified in the Collection having one or more of these associations. The entry for each writer contains the following information to the extent applicable and available:

1. *Biographical note*—Writer's name, years of birth and death, type of writer (poet, novelist, etc.), New England associations;
2. *Books by the writer*—Title and subtitle; co-author; editor; information about preface, foreword, introduction, notes, epilogue, illustrations, bibliography, discography; volume number; place of publication; publisher; year of publication; final page number; and for reprinted books, year of publication or copyright of edition reprinted;
3. *Books about the writer*—Author, co-author, editor, title and subtitle, and further information as listed above under "Books by the writer."

There are sure to be writers that I have missed in the total Collection of 3500 titles. About 200 writers are listed here, with approximately 625 books by them. Another 125 books are listed by authors of all races that are about the writers with New England connections.

I have taken the term "book" to mean not only the usual idea of "book-length," but also any publication of any length that has appeared, originally or in reprint, in individual, separate form; that is, not part of a larger assemblage such as a periodical or anthology. Thus Section I contains "book-length books" and sermons, addresses, lectures, speeches, tracts, treatises, brief narratives, chapbooks of poems, exhibition catalogs, walking-tour guides, and reprinted articles.

Exceptions to this definition of a "book," for reasons of their importance, are these entries: (1) Paul Cuffe, *Journal* and *Letters*, made available from manuscripts in Sheldon H. Harris, *Paul Cuffe: Black America and the African Return*; (2) Pauline E. Hopkins, *Hagar's Daughter, Of One Blood*, and *Winona*, novels that have appeared only serially in *The Colored American Magazine*; (3) Maria W. Stewart, *An Address* and *A Lecture*, reprinted conveniently from her *Productions* and the newspaper *The Liberator*, respectively, pieces that are by the first American woman to lecture in public on a political theme.

In Section II, "Afro-American Writers Associated with New England Not Represented with Books By or About Them in the Collection of Afro-American Literature," are listed about 80 additional writers having New England associations under the same criteria as for writers in Section I. A biographical note, with information of the same kind as in the earlier section, is provided. Once more, there are sure to be writers that I have overlooked.

The Collection of Afro-American Literature aims to gather the complete works of all black American writers, past and present, with New England connections. Readers are invited, with thanks, to send names of writers not listed in this book, along with any biographical and/or publishing information they may wish to include. Communications may be addressed to: Director, Collection of Afro-American Literature, Mildred F. Sawyer Library, Suffolk University, 8 Ashburton Place, Beacon Hill, Boston, Massachusetts 02108.

E.C.

BLACK WRITERS IN NEW ENGLAND

BOOKS BY AND ABOUT AFRO-AMERICAN WRITERS ASSOCIATED WITH NEW ENGLAND IN THE
Collection of Afro-American Literature

Allen, Samuel (b. 1917), poet, critic, editor. J.D., Harvard Law School, 1941; Prof. of English and Afro-American Literature, Boston Univ., 1971–81, retired; reads poetry and lectures on black history to students as member of School Volunteers for Boston.

Elfenbeinzähne (Ivory Tusks): Gedichte eines Afroamerikaners. By Paul Vesey [pseud.]. Ausgewählt und übertragen von Janheinz Jahn. Text in English and German. Heidelberg: Wolfgang Rothe Verlag, 1956. 47p.

Ivory Tusks and Other Poems by Paul Vesey [pseud.]. Published by the Author, 1968. 32p.

Paul Vesey's Ledger. London: Paul Breman Limited, 1975. 20p.

Ed., *Poems from Africa.* Drawings by Romare Bearden. New York: Crowell, 1973. 205p.

Samuel Allen

1

Allen, William G., biographer, editor. Studied law in Boston in 1842 or before.

Wheatley, Banneker, and Horton; With Selections from the Poetical Works of Wheatley and Horton. 1849 ed.; rpt. Freeport, N.Y.: Books for Libraries Press, 1970. 48p.

Asher, Jeremiah (b. 1812), memoirist. Born in North Brandford, Conn., attended district school to age twelve; farmhand; servant in white family, Hartford; pastor, Baptist church, Providence, R.I., 1841–49.

Incidents in the Life of the Rev. J. Asher, Pastor of Shiloh (Coloured) Baptist Church, Philadelphia, U.S.; and a Concluding Chapter of Facts Illustrating the Unrighteous Prejudice Existing in the Minds of American Citizens Toward Their Coloured Brethren. 1850 ed.; rpt. Freeport, N.Y.: Books for Libraries Press, 1971. 80p.

Barbour, Floyd B. (b. 1938), editor, playwright, short story writer. B.A., Bowdoin College, 1960; Assoc. Prof. of English and Director of Afro-American Studies, Simmons College, Boston.

Ed., *The Black Power Revolt: A Collection of Essays.* Bibliog. Boston: Porter Sargent, 1968. 287p.

Ed., *The Black Seventies.* Bibliog. Boston: Porter Sargent, 1970. 335p.

Barksdale, Richard (b. 1915), editor, critic. Born in Winchester, Mass.; B.A., Bowdoin College, 1937; Ph.D., Harvard Univ., 1951.

Ed., *Black Writers of America.* With Keneth Kinnamon. Bibliog. New York: Macmillan, 1972. 917p.

Langston Hughes. Bibliog. Chicago: American Library Association, 1977. 155p.

Beckham, Barry (b. 1944), novelist, editor. B.A., Brown Univ., 1966; Assoc. Prof. of English, Brown Univ.

Ed., *The Black Student's Guide to Colleges.* New York: Dutton, 1982. 336p.

Double Dunk. Los Angeles: Holloway House, 1980. 250p.

My Main Mother. New York: Walker, 1969. 214p.

Runner Mack. New York: Morrow, 1972. 213p.

Bibb, Henry (1815–1854), editor, author of slave narrative. Born a slave of slave mother in Kentucky; escaped, recaptured, and escaped several times, 1837–41; last owner an Indian; spent winter, 1846–47, in New England in antislavery work.

Narrative of the Life and Adventures of Henry Bibb, An American Slave, Written by Himself. 1849 ed.; rpt. in Gilbert Osofsky, ed., *Puttin' On Ole Massa: The Slave Narratives of Henry Bibb, William Wells Brown, and Solomon Northup* (New York: Harper and Row, 1969), p. 51–171. 1850 ed.; rpt. New York: Negro Universities Press, 1969. 204p.

Billingsley, Andrew (b. 1926), sociological essayist. M.S., Boston Univ., 1956; Ph.D., Brandeis Univ., 1964.

Black Families in White America. With assistance of Amy Tate Billingsley. Illus. Bibliog. Englewood Cliffs, N.J.: Prentice-Hall, 1968. 218p.

Blassingame, John W. (b. 1940), historian, editor. M. Phil., 1968, Ph.D., 1971, Yale Univ.; Prof. of History and Chairman, Program of Afro-American Studies, Yale Univ.

Ed., *Antislavery Newspapers and Periodicals.* Vols. 1–5 (1817–71). With Mae G. Henderson and Jessica M. Dunn. Illus. Boston: G.K. Hall, 1980–84. 2770p.

Ed., *The Frederick Douglass Papers: Series One, Speeches, Debates, and Interviews.* Vol. 1 (1841–46), 530p.; Vol. 2 (1847–54), 613p. With other editors. Illus. New Haven and London: Yale Univ. Press, 1979, 1982.

Frederick Douglass, the Clarion Voice. Illus. Bibliog. Washington, D.C.: Division of Publications, National Park Service, U.S. Dept. of the Interior, 1976. 72p.

Long Memory: The Black Experience in America. With Mary Frances Berry. Illus. Bibliog. New York: Oxford Univ. Press, 1982. 486p.

Ed., *New Perspectives on Black Studies.* Bibliog. Urbana: Univ. of Illinois Press, 1973. 243p.

The Slave Community: Plantation Life in the Antebellum South. Illus. Bibliog. New York: Oxford Univ. Press, 1972. 262p.

Ed., *Slave Testimony: Two Centuries of Letters, Speeches, Interviews, and Autobiographies.* Baton Rouge: Louisiana State Univ. Press, 1977. 777p.

About John W. Blassingame

Gilmore, Al-Tony, ed. *Revisiting Blassingame's "The Slave Community": The Scholars Respond.* Westport, Conn.: Greenwood Press, 1978. 206p.

Boles, Robert (b. 1943), novelist, short story writer. Has lived on Cape Cod and in Boston.

Curling. A novel. Boston: Houghton Mifflin, 1968. 259p.

The People One Knows. A novel. Boston: Houghton Mifflin, 1964. 177p.

Bontemps, Arna (1902–1973), poet, novelist, playwright, critic, biographer, anthologist. Curator, James Weldon Johnson Memorial Collection of Negro Arts and Letters, Yale Univ., 1969–73.

Ed., *American Negro Poetry.* 1st ed.; New York: Hill and Wang, 1963. 197p.

Ed., *American Negro Poetry.* Rev. ed.; New York: Hill and Wang, 1974. 231p.

Anyplace But Here. With Jack Conroy. Revised and expanded version of *They Seek a City.* Bibliog. New York: Hill and Wang, 1966. 372p.

Arna Bontemps-Langston Hughes Letters, 1925–1967. Ed. by Charles H. Nichols. Illus. Bibliog. New York: Dodd, Mead, 1980. 529p.

Black Thunder. Intro. for this ed. by the author. Boston: Beacon Press, 1968. 224p.

Chariot in the Sky: A Story of the Jubilee Singers. c1951; rpt. New York: Holt, Rinehart and Winston, 1971. 238p.

Drums at Dusk. A novel. Illus. Photocopy from microfilm of 1939 ed.; Ann Arbor, Mich.: University Microfilms, 1970. 226p.

Famous Negro Athletes. Illus. New York: Dodd, Mead, 1964. 155p.

The Fast Sooner Bound. With Jack Conroy. Illus. by Virginia Lee Burton. Boston: Houghton Mifflin, 1942. 28p.

Free At Last: The Life of Frederick Douglass. New York: Dodd, Mead, 1971. 310p.

God Sends Sunday. 1931 ed.; rpt. New York: AMS Press, 1972. 199p.

Ed., *Golden Slippers: An Anthology of Negro Poetry for Young Readers.* With biographies. Drawings by Henrietta Bruce Sharon. New York and London: Harper and Brothers, 1941. 220p.

Ed., *Great Slave Narratives.* Boston: Beacon Press, 1969. 331p.

Ed., *The Harlem Renaissance Remembered: Essays.* With memoir by Arna Bontemps. Illus. Bibliog. New York: Dodd, Mead, 1972. 310p.

Ed., *Hold Fast to Dreams: Poems Old and New.* Chicago: Follett Publishing Co., 1969. 192p.

Lonesome Boy. Illus. by Feliks Topolski. Boston: Houghton Mifflin, 1955. 28p.

Ed., *Negro American Heritage.* Illus. San Francisco: Century Communications, for Century Consultants, Chicago, 1968. 136p.

The Old South: "A Summer Tragedy" and Other Stories of the Thirties. New York: Dodd, Mead, 1973. 238p.

100 Years of Negro Freedom. Illus. Bibliog. New York: Dodd, Mead, 1961. 276p.

Personals. Poems. London: Paul Breman, 1963. 44p.

Ed., *The Poetry of the Negro, 1746–1970: An Anthology.* With Langston Hughes. Rev. ed.; Garden City, N.Y.: Doubleday, 1970. 645p.

Sad-faced Boy. Illus. by Virginia Lee Burton. Boston: Houghton Mifflin, 1937. 118p.

Story of the Negro. Illus. by Raymond Lufkin. New York: A.A. Knopf, 1948. 239p.

They Seek a City. With Jack Conroy. New York: Doubleday, Doran, 1945. 266p.

We Have Tomorrow. Illus. with photos by Marian Palfi. Boston: Houghton Mifflin, 1945. 131p.

Young Booker: Booker T. Washington's Early Days. Illus. New York: Dodd, Mead, 1972. 196p.

About Arna Bontemps

Fleming, Robert E. *James Weldon Johnson and Arna Wendell Bontemps: A Reference Guide.* Boston: G.K. Hall, 1978. 149p.

Braithwaite, William Stanley (1878–1962), poet, critic, anthologist, novelist. Born in Boston, lived much of his life in or near there; regular contributor of literary criticism to *Boston Evening Transcript.*

Ed., *Anthology of Magazine Verse for 1914.* New York: Gomme and Marshall, 1915. 296p.

Ed., *Anthology of Magazine Verse for 1916.* New York: Laurence J. Gomme, 1916. 266p.

Ed., *Anthology of Magazine Verse for 1919.* Boston: Small, Maynard and Co., 1919. 320p.

Ed., *Anthology of Magazine Verse for 1927.* Boston: B.J. Brimmer Co., 1927. 405p.

Ed., *The Book of Georgian Verse.* Vols. 13–14. 1908 ed.; rpt. Freeport, N.Y.: Books for Libraries Press, 1969. 1313p.

The House of Falling Leaves, with Other Poems. 1908 ed.; rpt. Miami, Fla.: Mnemosyne Publishing Co., 1969. 112p.

Lyrics of Life and Love. Illus. Boston: H.B. Turner and Co., 1904. 80p.

Selected Poems. 1948 ed.; rpt. Ann Arbor, Mich.: University Microfilms, 1975. 96p.

Ed., *Victory! Celebrated by Thirty-Eight American Poets.* Intro. by Theodore Roosevelt. Boston: Small, Maynard and Co., 1919. 84p.

About William Stanley Braithwaite

Butcher, Philip, ed. *The William Stanley Braithwaite Reader.* Illus. Incl. list of books by W.S.B. Ann Arbor: Univ. of Michigan Press, 1972. 322p.

Branch, William Blackwell (b. 1929), playwright. Born in New Haven, Conn.; resident fellow, Yale Univ., 1965–66.

A Medal for Willie. c1951; in Woodie King and Ron Milner, eds., *Black Drama Anthology* (New York: New American Library, 1972), p. 439–473.

In Splendid Error. c1953 under title *Frederick Douglass*; in James V. Hatch, editor, and Ted Shine, consultant, *Black Theater U.S.A.: Forty-Five Plays by Black Americans, 1847–1974* (New York: Free Press, 1974), p. 585–617.

Brawley, Benjamin (1882–1939), essayist, historian, poet. M.A., Harvard Univ., 1908; pastor, Messiah Baptist Church, Brockton, Mass., 1921–22.

Ed., *Early Negro American Writers: Selections with Biographical and Critical Introductions.* Bibliog. 1935 ed.; rpt. New York: Dover Publications, 1970. 305p.

History of Morehouse College: Written on the Authority of the Board of Trustees. Illus. c1917; rpt. College Park, Md.: McGrath Publishing Co., 1970. 218p.

Negro Builders and Heroes. Illus. Bibliog. Chapel Hill: Univ. of North Carolina Press, 1937. 315p.

The Negro Genius: A New Appraisal of the Achievement of the American Negro in Literature and the Fine Arts. Illus. Bibliog. c1937; rpt. New York: Dodd, Mead, 1966. 366p.

The Negro in Literature and Art in the United States. Illus. Bibliog. 1930 ed.; rpt. New York: AMS Press, 1971. 231p.

Paul Laurence Dunbar: Poet of His People. Bibliog. 1936 ed.; rpt. Port Washington, N.Y.: Kennikat Press, 1967. 159p.

A Short History of the American Negro. Illus. Bibliog. 4th rev. ed., 1939; rpt. New York: Macmillan, 1946. 288p.

A Social History of the American Negro: Being a History of the Negro Problem in the United States, Including a History and Study of the Republic of Liberia. Intro. by C. Eric Lincoln. Bibliog. 1921 ed.; rpt. New York: Johnson Reprint Corp., 1968. 420p.

Brooke, Edward W. (b. 1919), political essayist. LL.B., 1948, LL.M., 1949, Boston Univ. Law School; attorney, Boston, then Attorney General of Mass., 1963–67, U.S. Senator, 1967–79.

The Challenge of Change: Crisis in Our Two-Party System. Bibliog. Boston: Little, Brown, 1966. 269p.

About Edward W. Brooke

Cutler, John Henry. *Ed Brooke: Biography of a Senator.* Illus. Bibliog. Indianapolis: Bobbs-Merrill, 1972. 430p.

Brown, Sterling A. (b. 1901), poet, critic. B.A., Williams College, 1922; M.A., Harvard Univ., 1923.

The Collected Poems of Sterling A. Brown. Selected by Michael S. Harper. New York: Harper and Row, 1980. 257p.

The Last Ride of Wild Bill, and Eleven Narrative Poems. Detroit: Broadside Press, 1975. 53p.

Ed., *The Negro Caravan: Writings by American Negroes.* With Arthur P. Davis and Ulysses Lee. c1941; rpt. New York: Arno Press, 1969. 1082p.

Southern Road: Poems. Drawings by E. Simms Campbell. New York: Harcourt, Brace, 1932. 135p.

About Sterling A. Brown

Sterling A. Brown: A UMUM Tribute. Ed. by Black History Museum Committee. Bibliog. Philadelphia: Black History Museum UMUM Publishers, 1976. 106p.

Brown, William J. (b. 1814), autobiographer. Born in Providence, R.I., lived there as soapmaker, shoemaker, and minister of Meeting House Baptist Society.

The Life of William J. Brown, of Providence, R.I.; With Personal Recollections of Incidents in Rhode Island. 1883 ed.; rpt. Freeport, N.Y.: Books for Libraries Press, 1971. 230p.

Brown, William Wells (1814?–1884), novelist, playwright, essayist, historian. An escaped slave from Missouri, lived in Boston and vicinity from 1847, except for years 1849–54 spent in Great Britain; agent for Massachusetts and American Anti-Slavery societies; after Civil War, a practicing physician and temperance lecturer.

The Black Man; His Antecedents, His Genius, and His Achievements. "Memoir of the Author," p. 11–30. 1865 ed.; rpt. Miami, Fla.: Mnemosyne Publishing Co., 1969. 312p.

Clotelle; or, The Colored Heroine: A Tale of the Southern States. Illus. 1867 ed.; rpt. Miami, Fla.: Mnemosyne Publishing Co., 1969. 114p.

Clotel; or, The President's Daughter: A Narrative of Slave Life in the United States. Intro. by Arthur Davis. 1853 ed.; rpt. New York: Collier Books, 1970. 202p.

My Southern Home; or, The South and Its People. Illus. 1880 ed.; rpt. New York: Negro Universities Press, 1969. 253p.

Narrative of William W. Brown, A Fugitive Slave, Written by Himself.
Illus. Boston: Published at the Anti-Slavery Office, 1847; rpt. New York:
Johnson Reprint Corp., 1970. 110p. Rpt. in Gilbert Osofsky, ed., *Puttin'
On Ole Massa: The Slave Narratives of Henry Bibb, William Wells
Brown, and Solomon Northup* (New York: Harper and Row, 1969),
p. 172–223.

The Negro in the American Rebellion. Intro. and annotated by William
Edward Farrison. 1867 ed.; rpt. New York: Citadel Press, 1971. 389p.

*The Rising Son; or, The Antecedents and Advancement of the Colored
Race.* Illus. 1874 ed.; rpt. New York: Negro Universities Press,
1970. 552p.

*Sketches of Places and People Abroad: The American Fugitive in
Europe.* Illus. c1854; rpt. Freeport, N.Y.: Books for Libraries Press, 1970.
320p.

About William Wells Brown

Ellison, Curtis W. and **E.W. Metcalf, Jr.** *William Wells Brown and Martin
R. Delany: A Reference Guide.* Boston: G.K. Hall, 1978. 276p.

Farrison, William Edward. *Williams Wells Brown: Author and Reformer.*
Illus. Bibliog. Chicago: Univ. of Chicago Press, 1969. 482p.

Heermance, J. Noel. *William Wells Brown and Clotelle: A Portrait of the
Artist in the First Negro Novel.* Illus. Bibliog. Hamden, Conn.: Archon
Books, 1969. 107p.

Browne, Martha Griffith (d. 1906), autobiographer. Born a slave in Kentucky
of mulatto mother and white father; freed in owner's will with legacy of
$4000 and request to live in North; settled, probably in 1850's, in "quiet
puritanical little town in Massachusetts," teaching "small school of
African children."

Autobiography of a Female Slave. 1857 ed.; rpt. New York: Negro
Universities Press, 1969. 401p.

Butcher, Margaret Just (b. 1913), cultural historian. Ph.D., Boston Univ.,
1947.

The Negro in American Culture. Based on materials left by Alain Locke.
2nd ed.; New York: Knopf, 1972. 313p.

Capdeville, Annetta Elam (b. 1925), poet. Born in Boston, raised and
educated in Roxbury section; has been singer, actress, church worker,
and youth advisor.

My Soul Sings: Lyrics. Illus. Washington, D.C.: The Author, 1978. 34p.

Cass, Melnea A. (1896–1978), oral history memoirist. Attended grammar school in Newburyport, Mass., settled permanently in Boston in 1914; leader in numerous volunteer organizations.

Interview with Melnea A. Cass: February 1, 1977. Conducted by Tahi Lani Mottl. Illus. Cambridge, Mass.: Schlesinger Library, Radcliffe College, 1982. 140p.

Childress, Alice (b. 1920), playwright, novelist. Member, Radcliffe Institute, 1966–68.

Ed., *Black Scenes.* Bibliog. Garden City, N.Y.: Zenith Books, 1971. 154p.

A Hero Ain't Nothin' but a Sandwich. New York: Coward, McCann and Geoghegan, 1973. 126p.

Let's Hear It for the Queen: A Play. Illus. by Loring Eutemey. New York: Coward, McCann and Geoghegan, 1976. 47p.

Rainbow Jordan. New York: Coward, McCann and Geoghegan, 1981. 142p.

A Short Walk. New York: Coward, McCann and Geoghegan, 1979. 333p.

When the Rattlesnake Sounds: A Play. Drawings by Charles Lilly. New York: Coward, McCann and Geoghegan, 1975. 32p.

Wine in the Wilderness. c1969; in James V. Hatch, editor, and Ted Shine, consultant, *Black Theater U.S.A.: Forty-Five Plays by Black Americans, 1847–1974* (New York: Free Press, 1974), p. 737–755.

Cole, Maria (b. 1926), biographer. Spent youth in Boston area, attended Boston Clerical College.

Nat King Cole: An Intimate Biography. With Louie Robinson. Illus. Discography. New York: Morrow, 1971. 184p.

Cook, Mercer (b. 1903), critic, translator. B.A., Amherst College, 1925; M.A., 1931, Ph.D., 1936, Brown. Univ.

The Militant Black Writer in Africa and the United States. With Stepher E. Henderson. Bibliog. Madison: Univ. of Wisconsin Press, 1969. 136p.

Coombs, Orde (1939?–1984), essayist, editor. B.A., Yale Univ., 1965.

Do You See My Love for You Growing? New York: Dodd, Mead, 1972. 188p.

Drums of Life: A Photographic Essay on the Black Man in America. Photos by Chester Higgins, Jr. Text by Orde Coombs. Garden City, N.Y.: Anchor Press, 1974. 131p.

Some Time Ago: A Historical Portrait of Black Americans from 1850-1950. With Chester Higgins, Jr. Illus. Garden City, N.Y.: Anchor Press, 1980. 206p.

Ed., *We Speak as Liberators: Young Black Poets; An Anthology.* New York: Dodd, Mead, 1970. 252p.

Ed., *What We Must See: Young Black Storytellers; An Anthology.* New York: Dodd, Mead, 1971. 210p.

Cornish, Sam (b. 1935), poet, author of children's books. Taught in community-based schools in Boston; teaches writing and black literature, Emerson College, Boston; owns Fiction, Literature and the Arts Bookstore, Brookline, Mass., with specialty in Third World literature.

Generations: Poems. Pref. by Ruth Whitman. Boston: Beacon Press, 1971. 81p.

Grandmother's Pictures. Illus. by Jeanne Johns. Lenox, Mass.: Bookstore Press, 1974. 36p.

Your Hand in Mine. Illus. by Carl Owens. New York: Harcourt, Brace and World, 1970. 32p.

Corrothers, James D. (1869-1917), poet, journalist, autobiographer. Pastor, church of "coloured Baptists" in New England, possibly Haverhill, Mass., where preached before 1914.

The Black Cat Club: Negro Humor and Folklore. Illus. 1902 ed.; rpt. New York: AMS Press, 1972. 264p.

In Spite of the Handicap: An Autobiography. Intro. by Ray Stannard Baker. Illus. 1916 ed.; rpt. Westport, Conn.: Negro Universities Press, 1970. 238p.

Counter, S. Allen (b. 1944), essayist. Assoc. Prof. of Neuroscience, Harvard Medical School; Director, Harvard Foundation, Harvard Univ.

I Sought My Brother: An Afro-American Reunion. With David L. Evans. Illus. Cambridge, Mass.: M.I.T. Press, 1981. 276p.

Craft, William (b. 1824?), author of slave narrative. Went as fugitive slave with wife Ellen (1826-1891?) in disguise as his master from Georgia to Boston in 1849; were remarried by Theodore Parker in "Free Boston"; lived there, addressing antislavery meetings in New England, until passage of Fugitive Slave Act in 1850; sought by slavehunters who were resisted by Bostonians; took refuge in England.

Running a Thousand Miles for Freedom: or, The Escape of William and Ellen Craft from Slavery. Illus. Bibliog. 1860 ed.; rpt. New York: Arno Press, 1969. 111p. Rpt. in Arna Bontemps, ed. *Great Slave Narratives* (Boston: Beacon Press, 1969), p. 269-331.

Sterling, Dorothy. *Black Foremothers: Three Lives.* Intro. by Margaret Walker. Illus. by Judith Eloise Hooper. Bibliog. Old Westbury, N.Y.: Feminist Press, 1979. 167p.

Crite, Allan Rohan (b. 1910), artist historian, essayist, autobiographer. Has lived almost entire life in Boston; Diploma, School of Museum of Fine Arts, 1936; B.A., Harvard Univ., 1968; Illustrator, Technical Equipment, Boston Naval Shipyard, 1940–71.

All Glory: Brush Drawing Meditations on the Prayer of Consecration. Cambridge, Mass.: Society of Saint John the Evangelist, 1947. 28p.

An Artist's Sketchbook of the South End: A Walking Tour About Black People. Boston: Museum of Afro-American History, 1977. 40p.

An Autobiographical Sketch. Illus. Unpublished MS, 1976. n. pag.

Basic Forms, Part I: A Way of "Writing" Pictures. Illus. Unpublished MS, 1977–82. n. pag.

Basic Forms, Part II: Perspective. Illus. Unpublished MS, 1977–82. n. pag.

Basic Forms, Part III: The Body. Illus. Unpublished MS, 1981–82, n. pag.

The China Tour: A Journal of Community Leaders' Tour to China, 9–25 November, 1983. Illus. Unpublished MS, 1983. n. pag.

Commentaries: Whose Body Is This? Illus. Unpublished MS. Vol. 1 (1980–81), 161p.; Vol. 2 (1981), n. pag.

Is It Nothing to You? Illus. Department of Social Service, Episcopal Diocese of Massachusetts, 1 Joy St., Boston, MA 02108. 1948. 14p.

Random Commentaries: The African Connection. Part I, Presentation, 1981, n. pag.; *Part II, A Pilgrimage,* 1981, 71p.; *Part III, The Black Image,* 1982, n. pag.; *Part IV, The Black Image: A Visual Experience,* 1982, n. pag. Illus. Unpublished MS.

Random Commentaries: Whose Body. Illus. Unpublished MS, 1981. n. pag.

A Symbolic History of the American Negro, ed. by Donald Joseph. Illus. by Allan Crite. Boston, 1950. 36p.

Illus., *Three Spirituals from Earth to Heaven.* Cambridge, Mass.: Harvard Univ. Press, 1948. 165p.

Towards a Rediscovery of the Cultural Heritage of the United States. Illus. Boston: Boston Athenaeum, 1968. 23p.

Illus., *Were You There when They Crucified my Lord: A Negro Spiritual in Illustrations.* Cambridge, Mass.: Harvard Univ. Press, 1944. 93p.

Clark, Edward. *Annamae Palmer Crite and Allan Rohan Crite: Mother and Artist Son—An Interview.* Illus. Rpt. from *Melus: The Journal of the Society for the Study of the Multi-Ethnic Literature of the United States,* Vol. 6, No. 4 (Winter 1979), p. 67–78. The Author, 145 Allston St., Medford, MA 02155.

Rushing, Byron. *The Lost and Found Paintings of Allan Rohan Crite.* Exhibition catalog with comments by Allan Rohan Crite. Boston: Museum of Afro-American History, 1982. 8p.

Crummell, Alexander (1819–1898), essayist, speaker. Along with Henry Highland Garnet and two other black youths, enrolled in newly opened Noyes Academy, New Canaan, N.H., 1834; blacks forced to leave after few months when some 300 angry men with 90–100 oxen dragged the building into a swamp. Studied privately with Episcopal clergymen in Boston and Providence, R.I., 1839–43; tried unsuccessfully in 1844 to organize mission church among blacks in Providence.

The Future of Africa; being Addresses, Sermons, etc., Delivered in the Republic of Liberia. 1862 ed.; rpt. New York: Negro Universities Press, 1969. 354p.

Works of Alexander Crummell. Millwood, N.Y.: KTO Microform, 197? Microfilm, 12 reels, 35mm.

Cuffe, Paul (1759–1817), essayist, journal keeper, letter writer. Born on Cuttyhunk Island, Mass., of Indian mother and black father, former slave; spent most of life, when not at sea, in Westport, Mass., where joined Society of Friends; petitioned legislature and Dartmouth selectmen for rights of "Negroes and mulattoes"; in 1815 transported thirty-eight blacks in his brig *Traveller* to Sierra Leone to colonize as solution to limitations of life in America.

A Brief Account of the Settlement and Present Situation of the Colony of Sierra Leone, in Africa; As Communicated by Paul Cuffe (A Man of Colour) To His Friend in New York: Also, An Explanation of the Object of His Visit, and Some Advice to the People of Colour in the United States. 1812 ed.; rpt. in Sheldon H. Harris, *Paul Cuffe: Black America and the African Return* (New York: Simon and Schuster, 1972), p. 266–271; Dorothy Porter, *Early Negro Writing 1760–1837* (Boston: Beacon Press, 1971), p. 256–261.

Journal. In Harris, *Paul Cuffe: Black America and the African Return,* p. 77–158.

Letters. In Harris, *Paul Cuffe: Black America and the African Return,* p. 159–262.

(Whaling Museum, New Bedford, Mass.)

About Paul Cuffe

Harris, Sheldon H. *Paul Cuffe: Black America and the African Return.*
Illus. Bibliog. New York: Simon and Schuster, 1972. 288p.

The History of Prince Lee Boo, To Which is Added, The Life of Paul Cuffee, A Man of Colour, Also, Some Account of John Sackhouse, the Esquimaux. 1820 ed.; rpt. Miami, Fla.: Mnemosyne Publishing Co., 1969. 180p.; *The Life of Paul Cuffee,* p. 148–170.

Cullen, Countee (1903–1946), poet, novelist, playwright, anthologist. M.A., Harvard Univ., 1926.

The Black Christ and Other Poems. Decorations by Charles Cullen. 1929 ed.; Xerox facsimile, Ann Arbor, Mich.: University Microfilms, 1975. 110p.

Ed., *Caroling Dusk: An Anthology of Verse by Negro Poets.* Decorations by Aaron Douglas. New York and London: Harper, 1927. 237p.

Color. Poems. c1925; rpt. New York: Arno Press, 1969. 108p.

Copper Sun. Poems. Decorations by Charles Cullen. 1927 ed.; Xerox facsimile, Ann Arbor, Mich.: University Microfilms, 1975. 89p.

On These I Stand: An Anthology of the Best Poems of Countee Cullen. Selected by himself and including six new poems never before published. New York and London: Harper, 1947. 197p.

One Way to Heaven. 1932 ed.; rpt. New York: AMS Press, 1975. 280p.

About Countee Cullen

Bronz, Stephen H. *Roots of Negro Racial Consciousness; the 1920's: Three Harlem Renaissance Authors.* Bibliog. New York: Libra, 1964. 101p.

Ferguson, Blanche E. *Countee Cullen and the Negro Renaissance.* Illus. Bibliog. New York: Dodd, Mead, 1966. 213p.

Perry, Margaret. *A Bio-Bibliography of Countee P. Cullen, 1903–1946.* Foreword by Don M. Wolfe. Westport, Conn.: Greenwood Publishing Corp., 1971. 134p.

Turner, Darwin T. *In a Minor Chord: Three Afro-American Writers and Their Search for Identity.* Pref. by Harry T. Moore. Bibliog. Carbondale: Southern Illinois Univ. Press, 1971. 153p.

Davis, Allison (b. 1902), sociological essayist. B.A., Williams College, 1924; M.A. Harvard Univ., 1925.

Children of Bondage: The Personality Development of Negro Youth in the Urban South. With John Dollard. Prepared for American Youth Commission. Washington, D.C.: American Council on Education, 1940. 299p.

Leadership, Love, and Aggression. Bibliog. San Diego and New York: Harcourt Brace Jovanovich, 1983. 260p.

Davis, Angela (b. 1944), essayist, autobiographer. B.A., Brandeis Univ., 1965.

If They Come in the Morning: Voices of Resistance. With others. Foreword by Julian Bond. New York: New American Library, 1971. 288p.

About Angela Davis

A Political Biography of Angela Davis. Los Angeles: National United Committee to Free Angela Davis, ca.1970. 8p.

Smith, Nelda J. and **Ruby E. White.** *From Where I Sat.* "A detailed account taken from the official transcript of the trial of Angela Y. Davis." New York: Vantage Press, 1973. 246p.

Davis, Charles T. (1918–1981), literary scholar, critic. B.A., Dartmouth College, 1939; Prof. of English and Chairman, Program of Afro-American Studies, Yale Univ., 1976–81.

Black Is the Color of the Cosmos: Essays on Afro-American Literature and Culture, 1942–1981. Ed. by Henry Louis Gates, Jr. Foreword by A. Bartlett Giamatti. Illus. Bibliog. New York: Garland Publishing, 1982. 376p.

Ed., *On Being Black: Writings by Afro-Americans from Frederick Douglass to the Present.* With Daniel Walden. Greenwich, Conn.: Fawcett Publications, 1970. 383p.

Richard Wright: A Primary Bibliography. With Michel Fabre. Boston: G. K. Hall, 1982. 232p.

Delany, Martin R. (1812–1885), editor, novelist, black nationalist essayist. Enrolled in medical school of Harvard College, November, 1850; fellow students protested his presence in their classes with petitions to medical faculty, which, headed by Oliver Wendell Holmes, allowed him to finish winter term but refused further study at Harvard.

Blake; or, The Huts of America. A novel. Intro. by Floyd J. Miller. Boston: Beacon Press, 1970. 321p.

The Condition, Elevation, Emigration, and Destiny of the Colored People of the United States. 1852 ed.; rpt. New York: Arno Press, 1968. 214p.

Official Report of the Niger Valley Exploring Party. In M. R. Delany and Robert Campbell, *Search for a Place: Black Separatism and Africa, 1860.* Intro. by Howard H. Bell. Ann Arbor: Univ. of Michigan Press, 1969. 250p.

About Martin R. Delany

Ellison, Curtis W. and **E. W. Metcalf, Jr.** *William Wells Brown and Martin R. Delany: A Reference Guide.* Boston: G. K. Hall, 1978. 276p.

Griffith, Cyril E. *The African Dream: Martin R. Delany and the Emergence of Pan-African Thought.* Bibliog. University Park: Pennsylvania State Univ. Press, 1975. 153p.

Rollin, Frank A. *Life and Public Services of Martin R. Delany.* 1883 ed.; rpt. New York: Arno Press, 1969. 367p.

Ullman, Victor. *Martin R. Delany: The Beginnings of Black Nationalism.* Bibliog. Boston: Beacon Press, 1971. 534p.

Dodson, Owen (b. 1914), playwright, poet, novelist, short story writer. B.A., Bates College, 1936; M.F.A. in Drama, Yale Univ., 1939.

Boy at the Window. A novel. c1951; rpt. Chatham, N.J.: Chatham Bookseller, 1972. 212p.

Come Home Early, Child. A novel. New York: Popular Library, 1977. 221p.

The Confession Stone: Song Cycles. London: P. Breman, 1971. 28p.

Powerful Long Ladder. Poems. New York: Farrar, Strauss, 1946. 103p.

Douglass, Frederick (1817?–1895), autobiographer, speaker, journalist. After escape from slavery in Maryland, lived in New Bedford, Mass., 1838–42, Lynn, 1842–45; became agent-lecturer for Massachusetts Anti-Slavery Society following impromptu speech at abolitionist gathering in Nantucket, 1841; in Civil War was recruiting agent for two colored Mass. regiments.

A Black Diplomat in Haiti: The Diplomatic Correspondence of U.S. Minister Frederick Douglass from Haiti, 1889–1891. Ed. and intro. by Norma Brown. Vol. 1, 268p.; Vol. 2, 256p. Facsimile. Salisbury, N.C.: Documentary Publications, 1977.

Dessalines, a Dramatic Tale: A Single Chapter from Haiti's History, by William Edgar Easton. Incl. oration of Frederick Douglass at dedication of Haitian pavilion at World's Fair, Chicago, 1893. Illus. Galveston, Texas: J. W. Burson Co., 1893. 138p.

Douglass' Monthly. 5 vols. in 2; Vol. 1–3 (1859–61), p. 1–464; Vol. 4–5 (1861–63), p. 465–862. Rpt. New York: Negro Universities Press, 1969.

Frederick Douglass on Women's Rights. Ed. and intro. by Philip S. Foner. Westport, Conn.: Greenwood Press, 1976. 190p.

The Frederick Douglass Papers: Series One, Speeches, Debates, and Interviews. Vol. 1 (1841–46), 530p.; Vol. 2 (1847–54), 613p. Ed. by John W. Blassingame and others. Illus. New Haven and London: Yale Univ. Press, 1979, 1982.

From Slave to Statesman: The Life and Times of Frederick Douglass. Abridgement of 1892 ed., *Life and Times of Frederick Douglass.* New York: Noble and Noble, 1972. 231p.

Life and Times of Frederick Douglass: His Early Life as a Slave, His Escape from Bondage, and His Complete History, Written by Himself. Intro. by Rayford W. Logan. Bibliog. 1892 ed.; rpt. New York: Collier Books, 1962. 640p.

The Life and Writings of Frederick Douglass. Ed. and intro. by Philip S. Foner. Illus. Bibliog. 4 vols. New York: International Publishers, 1950–55. 2046p.

The Mind and Heart of Frederick Douglass: Excerpts from Speeches of the Great Negro Orator. Adapted by Barbara Ritchie. New York: Crowell, 1968. 201p.

My Bondage and my Freedom. 1855 ed.; rpt. New York: Arno Press, 1968. 464p.

Narrative of the Life of Frederick Douglass, An American Slave, Written by Himself. Illus. 1st ed.; Boston: Anti-Slavery Office, 1845. 125p.

Narrative of the Life of Frederick Douglass, An American Slave, Written by Himself. Ed. and intro. by Benjamin Quarles. Illus. Map. 1845 ed.; rpt. Cambridge, Mass.: Belknap Press, 1960. 163p.

Narrative of the Life of Frederick Douglass, An American Slave, Written by Himself. Illus. Map. 1845 ed.; rpt. New York: New American Library, 1968. 126p.

About Frederick Douglass

Blassingame, John W. *Frederick Douglass, the Clarion Voice.* Illus. Bibliog. Washington, D.C.: Division of Publications, National Park Service, U.S. Dept. of the Interior, 1976. 72p.

Bontemps, Arna. *Free at Last: The Life of Frederick Douglass.* New York: Dodd, Mead, 1971. 310p.

Chesnutt, Charles Waddell. *Frederick Douglass.* Illus. Bibliog. Boston: Small, Maynard and Co., 1899. 141p.

Davis, Ossie. *Escape to Freedom: A Play About Young Frederick Douglass.* New York: Viking Press, 1978. 89p.

Douglass, Helen Pitts, ed. *In Memoriam: Frederick Douglass.* Illus. 1897 ed.; rpt. Freeport, N.Y.: Books for Libraries Press, 1971. 350p.

Graham, Shirley. *There Once Was a Slave: The Heroic Story of Frederick Douglass.* Bibliog. New York: J. Messner, 1947. 310p.

Gregory, James Monroe. *Frederick Douglass, the Orator: Containing an Account of His Life; His Eminent Public Services; His Brilliant Career as Orator; Selections from His Speeches and Writings.* Intro. by W. S. Scarborough. Illus. 1893 ed. with 3 chaps. added after Douglass' death; Springfield, Mass.: Willey Co., 189? 309p.

Holland, Frederick May. *Frederick Douglass: The Colored Orator.* Illus. 1891 ed.; rpt. Westport, Conn.: Negro Universities Press, 1970. 423p.

Huggins, Nathan Irvin. *Slave and Citizen: The Life of Frederick Douglass.* Bibliog. Boston: Little, Brown, 1980. 194p.

Preston, Dickson J. *Young Frederick Douglass: The Maryland Years.* Illus. Bibliog. Baltimore: Johns Hopkins Univ. Press, 1980. 242p.

Quarles, Benjamin, ed. *Frederick Douglass.* Bibliog. Englewood Cliffs, N.J.: Prentice-Hall, 1968. 184p.

Quarles, Benjamin. *Frederick Douglass.* A biography. New pref. by James M. McPherson. Illus. Bibliog. 1948 ed.; rpt. New York: Atheneum, 1969. 378p.

Sterling, Philip. *Four Took Freedom: The Lives of Harriet Tubman, Frederick Douglass, Robert Smalls, and Blanche K. Bruce.* Illus. by Charles White. Garden City, N.Y.: Doubleday, 1967. 116p.

Walker, Peter. *Moral Choices: Memory, Desire, and Imagination in Nineteenth-Century Abolition.* Illus. Bibliog. Baton Rouge: Louisiana State Univ. Press, 1978. 387p.

Washington, Booker T. *Frederick Douglass.* Bibliog. c1906; rpt. Westport, Conn.: Greenwood Press, 1969. 365p.

Dreer, Herman (b. 1889), novelist. B.A., Bowdoin College, 1910.

The Immediate Jewel of his Soul: A Romance. Illus. c1919; rpt. College Park, Md.: McGrath Publishing Co., 1969. 317p.

Du Bois, Shirley Graham (see also **Graham, Shirley**) (1906–1977), biographer, novelist. Julius Rosenwald Fellow, School of Drama, Yale Univ., 1938–40.

Du Bois: A Pictorial Biography. Chicago: Johnson Publishing Co., 1978. 174p.

Gamal Abdel Nasser, Son of the Nile: A Biography. Illus. Bibliog. New York: Third Press, 1972. 250p.

His Day Is Marching On: A Memoir of W. E. B. Du Bois. Philadelphia: Lippincott, 1971. 384p.

Zulu Heart. A novel. New York: Third Press, 1974. 235p.

Du Bois, W. E. B. (William Edward Burghardt) (1868–1963), essayist, historian, editor, speaker, novelist, poet, autobiographer. Born and raised in Great Barrington, Mass.; B.A., 1890, M.A., 1891, Ph.D., 1895, Harvard Univ.

An ABC of Color: Selections Chosen by the Author from Over a Half Century of His Writings. Intro. by John Oliver Killens. New York: International Publishers, 1969. 215p.

Africa, Its Geography, People, and Products and *Africa, Its Place in Modern History.* Intro. by Herbert Aptheker. 1930 ed.; rpt. Millwood, N.Y.: KTO Press, 1977. 69p.

Ed., *Atlanta University Publications.* Vol. 1, Nos. 1–6 (1896–1901), 374p.; Vol. 2, Nos. 7–11 (1902–1906), 582p. 1896–1906 ed.; rpt. New York: Octagon Books, 1968.

The Autobiography of W. E. B. Du Bois: A Soliloquy on Viewing My Life from the Last Decade of Its First Century. Illus. Bibliog. New York: International Publishers, 1968. 448p.

Black Folk, Then and Now. Intro. by Herbert Aptheker. Maps. Bibliog. 1939 ed.; rpt. Millwood, N.Y.: Kraus-Thomson, 1975. 401p.

The Black North in 1901: A Social Study. New York Times, Nov.–Dec., 1901; rpt. New York: Arno Press, 1969. 46p.

Black Reconstruction in America: An Essay Toward a History of the Part Which Black People Played in the Attempt to Reconstruct Democracy in America, 1860–1880. Bibliog. c1935; rpt. New York: Atheneum, 1971. 746p.

Book Reviews by W. E. B. Du Bois. Comp. and ed. by Herbert Aptheker. Millwood, N.Y.: KTO Press, 1977. 263p.

Color and Democracy: Colonies and Peace. Illus. New York: Harcourt, Brace, 1945. 143p.

Contributions by W. E. B. Du Bois in Government Publications and Proceedings. Comp. and ed. by Herbert Aptheker. Illus. Millwood, N.Y.: Kraus-Thomson, 1980. 411p.

The Correspondence of W. E. B. Du Bois. Vol. 1, Selections (1877–1934), 507p.; Vol. 2 (1934–44), 419p.; Vol. 3 (1944–63), 483p. Illus. Bibliog. Amherst: Univ. of Massachusetts Press, 1973, 1976, 1978.

Darkwater: Voices from Within the Veil. 1920 ed.; rpt. New York: Schocken Books, 1969. 276p.

Dusk of Dawn: An Essay Toward an Autobiography of a Race Concept. 1940 ed.; rpt. New York: Schocken Books, 1968. 334p.

The Education of Black People: Ten Critiques, 1906–1960. Ed. by Herbert Aptheker. Amherst: Univ. of Massachusetts Press, 1973. 171p.

The Emerging Thought of W. E. B. Du Bois: Essays and Editorials from "The Crisis." Intro., commentaries, and personal memoir by Henry Lee Moon. New York: Simon and Schuster, 1972. 440p.

The Gift of Black Folk: The Negroes in the Making of America. Intro. by Edward F. McSweeney. Boston: Stratford Co., 1924. 349p.

In Battle for Peace: The Story of My 83rd Birthday. With comment by Shirley Graham. New York: Masses and Mainstream, 1952. 192p.

John Brown. New foreword by Blyden Jackson. Illus. Bibliog. 1909 ed.; rpt. Northbrook, Ill.: Metro Books, 1972. 406p.

Mansart Builds a School. His *The Black Flame, A Trilogy,* Book Two. New York: Mainstream Publishers, 1959. 367p.

The Negro. New intro. by George Shepperson. Bibliog. Maps. 1915 ed.; rpt. London and New York: Oxford Univ. Press, 1970. 157p.

The Negro. New intro. by Herbert Aptheker. Bibliog. Maps. 1915 ed.; rpt. Millwood, N.Y.: Kraus-Thomson, 1975. 262p.

Ed., *The Negro American Family: Report of a Social Study Made Principally by the College Classes of 1909 and 1910 of Atlanta University, Under the Patronage of the Trustees of the John F. Slater Fund; Togeteher with the Proceedings of the 13th Annual Conference for the Study of the Negro Problems, Held at Atlanta University on Tuesday, May the 26th, 1908.* Illus. Bibliog. 1908 ed.; rpt. New York: Negro Universities Press, 1969. 156p.

Ed., *The Negro Artisan: Report of a Social Study Made Under the Direction of Atlanta University; Together with the Proceedings of the Seventh Conference for the Study of the Negro Problems, Held at Atlanta University, on May 27th, 1902.* Bibliog. Atlanta, Ga.: Atlanta Univ. Press, 1902. 192p.

Ed., *The Negro in Business: Report of a Social Study Made Under the Direction of Atlanta University; Together with the Proceedings of the Fourth Conference for the Study of the Negro Problems, Held at Atlanta University, May 30-31, 1899.* 1899 ed.; rpt. New York: AMS Press, 1971. 77p.

The Ordeal of Mansart. His *The Black Flame, A Trilogy, Book One.* New York: Mainstream Publishers, 1957. 316p.

The Papers of W. E. B. Du Bois: 1803 (1877-1963) 1965. Sanford, N.C.: Microfilming Corp of America, 1980-81. Microfilm, 89 reels, 35 mm.

The Philadelphia Negro: A Social Study. Together with a special report on domestic service, by Isabel Eaton. Illus. 1899 ed.; rpt. New York: Schocken Books, 1967. 520p.

Prayers for Dark People. Ed. by Herbert Aptheker. Amherst: Univ. of Massachusetts Press, 1980. 75p.

The Quest of the Silver Fleece. A novel. Illus. by H. S. de Lay. 1911 ed.; rpt. Miami, Fla.: Mnemosyne Publishing Co., 1969. 434p.

Ed., *A Select Bibliography of the Negro American: A Compilation Made Under the Direction of Atlanta University; Together with the Proceedings of the Tenth Conference for the Study of the Negro Problems, Held at Atlanta University, on May 30, 1905.* Atlanta, Ga.: Atlanta Univ. Press, 1905. 71p.

Selected Poems by W. E. B. Du Bois. Foreword by Kwame Nkrumah. Exposition by Shirley Graham. Accra, Ghana: Ghana Universities Press, n.d. 42p.

Selections from "Phylon." Comp. and ed. by Herbert Aptheker. Millwood, N.Y.: Kraus-Thomson, 1980. 453p.

Selections from "The Brownies' Book." Comp. and ed. by Herbert Aptheker. Millwood, N.Y.: Kraus-Thomson, 1980. 159p.

Selections from "The Crisis." Comp. and ed. by Herbert Aptheker. 2 vols. Millwood, N.Y.: Kraus-Thomson, 1983. 782p.

The Seventh Son: The Thought and Writings of W. E. B. Du Bois. Ed. and intro. by Julius Lester. 2 vols. Bibliog. New York: Random House, 1971. 767p.

The Souls of Black Folk: Essays and Sketches. Intro. by Saunders Redding. Illus. 1903 ed.; rpt. New York: Dodd, Mead, 1979. 199p.

The Suppression of the African Slave-Trade to the United States of America, 1638–1870. New intro. by Philip S. Foner. Bibliog. 1896 ed.; rpt. New York: Dover Publications, 1970. 335p.

W. E. B. Du Bois: A Reader. Ed. and intro. by Meyer Weinberg. New York: Harper and Row, 1970. 471p.

W. E. B. Du Bois on Sociology and the Black Community. Ed. and intro. by Dan S. Green and Edwin D. Driver. Bibliog. Chicago: Univ. of Chicago Press, 1978. 320p.

W. E. B. Du Bois Speaks: Speeches and Addresses. Ed. by Philip S. Foner. 2 vols. New York: Pathfinder Press, 1970. 635p.

W. E. B. Du Bois: "The Crisis" Writings. Ed. and intro. by Daniel Walden. Bibliog. Greenwich, Conn.: Fawcett Publications, 1972. 447p.

The World and Africa: An Inquiry into the Part Which Africa Has Played in World History. Enl. ed., with new writings on Africa, 1955–61. Illus. Bibliog. New York: International Publishers, 1965. 352p.

Worlds of Color. His *The Black Flame, A Trilogy, Book Three.* New York: Mainstream Publishers, 1961. 349p.

Writings by W. E. B. Du Bois in Nonperiodical Literature Edited by Others. Collated and ed. by Herbert Aptheker. Millwood, N.Y.: Kraus-Thomson, 1982. 302p.

Writings by W. E. B. Du Bois in Periodicals Edited by Others. Collated and ed. by Herbert Aptheker. 4 vols. (1891–1961). Illus. Millwood, N.Y.: Kraus-Thomson, 1982. 1357p.

About W. E. B. Du Bois

Aptheker, Herbert. *Annotated Bibliography of the Published Writings of W. E. B. Du Bois.* Millwood, N.Y.: Kraus-Thomson, 1973. 626p.

Broderick, Francis L. *W. E. B. Du Bois, Negro Leader in a Time of Crisis.* Illus. Bibliog. Stanford, Calif.: Stanford Univ. Press, 1959. 259p.

Clarke, John Henrik, ed. *Black Titan: W. E. B. Du Bois.* Anthology by the editors of *Freedomways.* Bibliog. Boston: Beacon Press, 1970. 333p.

Du Bois, Shirley Graham. *Du Bois: A Pictorial Biography.* Chicago: Johnson Publishing Co., 1978. 174p.

-----------. *His Day Is Marching On: A Memoir of W. E. B. Du Bois.* Philadelphia: Lippincott, 1971. 384p.

Lacy, Leslie Alexander. *Cheer the Lonesome Traveler: The Life of W. E. B. Du Bois.* Illus. by James Barkley, and with photos. Bibliog. New York: Dial Press, 1970. 183p.

Logan, Rayford W., ed. *W. E. B. Du Bois: A Profile.* New York: Hill and Wang, 1971. 324p.

McDonnell, Robert W. *The Papers of W. E. B. Du Bois, 1803 (1877–1963) 1965: A Guide.* Sanford, N.C.: Micröfilming Corp. of America, 1981. 305p.

Moore, Jack B. *W. E. B. Du Bois.* Illus. Bibliog. Boston: Twayne Publishers, 1981. 185p.

Partington, Paul G. *W. E. B. Du Bois: A Bibliography of His Published Writings.* Rev. ed.; The Author, 7320 S. Gretna Ave., Whittier, CA 90606. 1979. 202p.

Rudwick, Elliott M. *W. E. B. Du Bois: Propagandist of the Negro Protest.* New pref. by Louis Harlan. Bibliog. Orig. pub. as *W. E. B. Du Bois: A Study in Minority Group Leadership.* 1960 ed.; rpt. New York: Atheneum, 1968. 390p.

––––––––––. *W. E. B. Du Bois: Voice of the Black Protest Movement.* With new epilogue. Bibliog. Orig. pub. as *W. E. B. Du Bois: A Study in Minority Group Leadership.* 1960 ed.; rpt. Urbana: Univ. of Illinois Press, 1982. 400p.

Salk, Erwin A. *Du Bois, Robeson, Two Giants of the 20th Century: The Story of an Exhibit and a Bibliography.* Illus. Chicago: Columbia College Press, 1977. 20p.

Sterling, Dorothy and **Benjamin Quarles.** *Lift Every Voice: The Lives of Booker T. Washington, W. E. B. Du Bois, Mary Church Terrell, and James Weldon Johnson.* Illus. by Ernest Crichlow. Garden City, N.Y.: Doubleday, 1965. 116p.

Sterne, Emma. *His Was the Voice: The Life of W. E. B. Du Bois.* Foreword by Ronald Stevenson. Illus. Bibliog. New York: Crowell-Collier Press, 1971. 232p.

Easton, Hosea, essayist, sermon writer. Minister in Hartford, Conn.; in 1837 gave proceeds of published essays and sermon to "a colored society in Hartford, Conn., who have lost their meeting-house by fire."

A Treatise on the Intellectual Character, and Civil and Political Condition of the Colored People of the U. States; and the Prejudice Exercised Towards Them: With a Sermon on the Duty of the Church to Them. Sermon is omitted in printing. 1837 ed.; rpt. in Dorothy Porter, *Negro Protest Pamphlets: A Compendium* (New York: Arno Press, 1969), 55p.

Edmonds, Randolph (b. 1900), playwright. Studied with General Education Board Fellowship in Dept. of Drama, Yale Univ., 1934.

The Land of Cotton, and Other Plays. 1942 ed.; Xerox facsimile, Ann Arbor, Mich.: University Microfilms, 1977. 267p.

Shades and Shadows. 1930 ed.; Xerox facsimile, Ann Arbor, Mich.: University Microfilms, 1977. 171p.

Six Plays for a Negro Theatre. Foreword by Frederick H. Koch. c1934; Xerox facsimile, Ann Arbor, Mich.: University Microfilms, 1979. 155p.

Elder, Lonne III (b. 1931), playwright. Attended School of Drama, Yale Univ.

Ceremonies in Dark Old Men. New York: Farrar, Straus and Giroux, 1969. 179p.

Eldridge, Elleanor (1784–1845?), oral history memoirist. Born in Warwick, R.I., of African and Indian blood; worked many years in Warwick and Providence as domestic for white families.

Memoirs of Elleanor Eldridge. [Told by Frances Harriet (Whipple) Greene McDougall (1805–1878)]. Illus. 2nd ed., 1843; rpt. Freeport, N.Y.: Books for Libraries Press, 1971. 127p.

Ellison, Ralph (b. 1914), novelist, short story writer, essayist. Was Visiting Fellow, Yale Univ.; taught at Bennington College.

The City in Crisis. With Whitney M. Young, Jr., and Herbert Gans. Intro. by Bayard Rustin. Illus. New York: A. Philip Randolph Educational Fund, 1970. 60p.

Invisible Man. New York: Random House, 1952. 439p.

Shadow and Act. New York: Random House, 1964. 317p.

The Writer's Experience. Lectures by Ralph Ellison and Karl Shapiro. Washington, D.C.: Library of Congress (for sale by Superintendent of Documents, U.S. Government Printing Office), 1964. 32p.

About Ralph Ellison

Covo, Jacqueline. *The Blinking Eye: Ralph Waldo Ellison and His American, French, German, and Italian Critics, 1952–1971; Bibliographic Essays and a Checklist.* Metuchen, N.J.: Scarecrow Press. 1974. 214p.

Dietze, Rudolf F. *Ralph Ellison: The Genesis of an Artist.* Bibliog. Nürnberg: H. Carl, 1982. 203p.

Gottesman, Ronald, ed. *The Merrill Studies in Invisible Man.* Bilbiog. Columbus, Ohio: Merrill Publishing Co., 1971. 120p.

Gysin, Fritz. *The Grotesque in American Negro Fiction: Jean Toomer, Richard Wright, and Ralph Ellison.* Bibliog. Bern, Switzerland: Francke, 1975. 330p.

Hersey, John, ed. *Ralph Ellison: A Collection of Critical Essays.* Bibliog. Englewood Clifs, N.J.: Prentice-Hall, 1974. 180p.

List, Robert N. *Dedalus in Harlem: The Joyce-Ellison Connection.* Bibliog. Washington, D.C.: University Press of America, 1982. 322p.

O'Meally, Robert G. *The Craft of Ralph Ellison.* Illus. Bibliog. Cambridge, Mass.: Harvard Univ. Press, 1980. 212p.

Reilly, John M., ed. *Twentieth Century Interpretations of Invisible Man: A Collection of Critical Essays.* Englewood Cliffs, N.J.: Prentice-Hall, 1970. 120p.

Trimmer, Joseph F., ed. *A Casebook on Ralph Ellison's Invisible Man.* New York: Crowell, 1972. 321p.

Evans, David L. (b. 1939), essayist. Senior Admissions Officer, Undergraduate Admissions, Harvard Univ.

I Sought My Brother: An Afro-American Reunion. With S. Allen Counter. Illus. Cambridge, Mass.: M.I.T. Press, 1981. 276p.

Fair, Ronald L. (b. 1932), novelist, poet. Taught at Wesleyan Univ., Conn.

Cornbread, Earl and Me. [Hog Butcher, 1966.] New York: Bantam Books, 1975. 201p.

Excerpts. Poems. London: Paul Breman Ltd., 1975. 20p.

Hog Butcher. New York: Harcourt, Brace and World, 1966. 182p.

Many Thousand Gone: An American Fable. c1965; rpt. Chatham, N.J.: Chatham Bookseller, 1973. 114p.

Rufus. Poems. Detroit: Lotus Press, 1980. 58p.

We Can't Breathe. New York: Harper and Row, 1972. 216p.

World of Nothing: Two Novellas. New York: Harper and Row, 1970. 133p.

Fields, Julia (b. 1938), poet. M.A., Breadloaf School of English, Middlebury College, 1973.

East of Moonlight. Illus. Charlotte, N.C.: Red Clay Books, 1973. 52p.

Fields, Karen (b. 1945), memoirist, essayist. B.A., Radcliffe College, 1967; Ph.D., Brandeis Univ., 1977; Instructor in Sociology, Boston Univ., 1975–77; Asst. Prof. of Sociology, 1977–83, Assoc. Prof., 1983––, Brandeis Univ.

Lemon Swamp and Other Places: A Carolina Memoir. By Mamie Garvin Fields with Karen Fields. Illus. New York: Free Press, 1983. 250p.

Fields, Mamie Garvin (b. 1888), oral history memoirist. Chambermaid for wealthy white woman in Winthrop Beach, Mass., and Boston, near Common, 1913; sewer in "sewing factory," dressmaker, Boston, 1913–14; lived in Roxbury section.

Lemon Swamp and Other Places: A Carolina Memoir. With Karen Fields. Illus. New York: Free Press, 1983. 250p.

Fisher, Rudolph (1897–1934), novelist, short story writer. Raised in Providence, R.I.; B.A., 1919, M.A., 1920, Brown Univ.

The Conjure-Man Dies: A Mystery Tale of Dark Harlem. Intro. by Stanley Ellin. c1932; rpt. New York: Arno Press, 1971. 316p.

The Walls of Jericho. Illus. c1928; rpt. New York: Arno Press, 1969. 307p.

Fleming, Ray (b. 1945), poet. M.A., Harvard Univ., 1973.

Diplomatic Relations: Poems. Detroit: Lotus Press, 1982. 59p.

Forbes, Calvin (b. 1945), poet. Taught at Emerson College, Boston, and Tufts Univ.

Blue Monday. Middletown, Conn.: Wesleyan Univ. Press, 1974. 63p.

Forman, James (b. 1928), social activist memoirist, biographer. Enrolled in African Research and Studies Program, Boston Univ., 1957–58; French Summer School, Middlebury College, 1960.

Ceremony of Innocence. New York: Hawthorn Books, 1970. 249p.

The Making of Black Revolutionaries: A Personal Account. New York: Macmillan, 1972. 568p.

Sammy Young, Jr.: The First Black College Student to Die in the Black Liberation Movement. Illus. New York: Grove Press, 1968. 262p.

Forten, Charlotte L. (1837–1914), journal keeper, poet. Graduated from Higginson Grammar School, Salem, Mass., 1855, Salem Normal School, 1856; taught in Epes Grammar School, Salem, 1856–58.

The Journal of Charlotte Forten: A Free Negro in the Slave Era. Ed. and intro. by Ray Allen Billington. Illus. Bibliog. New York: Collier Books, 1961. 286p.

Franklin, John Hope (b. 1915), historian. M.A., 1936, Ph.D., 1941, Harvard Univ.

Ed., *Black Leaders of the Twentieth Century.* With August Meier. Illus. Bilbiog. Urbana: Univ. of Illinois Press, 1982. 372p.

Ed., *Color and Race.* Bibliog. Boston: Beacon Press, 1969. 391p.

From Slavery to Freedom: A History of American Negroes. Illus. Bibliog. 1st ed.; New York: A. A. Knopf, 1947. 622p.

From Slavery to Freedom: A History of Negro Americans. Illus. Bibliog. 5th ed.; New York: Knopf, 1980. 554p.

George Washington Williams: The Massachusetts Years. Rpt. from *Proceedings of American Antiquarian Society,* Vol. 92, Part 2 (October 1982), p. 243–263. Worcester, Mass.: American Antiquarian Society, 1983.

An Illustrated History of Black Americans. With the editors of Time-Life Books. Bibliog. New York: Time-Life Books, 1973. 192p.

Land of the Free: A History of the United States. With John W. Caughey and Ernest R. May. Illus. Bibliog. New York: Benziger Bros., 1966. 658p.

Racial Equality in America. Bibliog. Chicago: Univ. of Chicago Press, 1976. 113p.

Reconstruction: After the Civil War. Illus. Bibliog. Chicago: Univ. of Chicago Press, 1961. 258p.

A Southern Odyssey: Travelers in the Antebellum North. Illus. Bibliog. Baton Rouge: Louisiana State Univ. Press, 1976. 299p.

Frazier, E. Franklin (1894–1962), sociological essayist. M.A., Clark Univ., 1920.

Black Bourgeoisie. Bibliog. Glencoe, Ill.: Free Press, 1957. 264p.

The Negro Church in America. Bibliog. New York: Schocken Books, 1964. 92p.

The Negro Family in the United States. Foreword by Nathan Glazer. Bibliog. Rev. and abridged ed., 1948; Chicago: Univ. of Chicago Press, 1966. 372p.

Negro Youth at the Crossways: Their Personality Development in the Middle States. Intro. by St. Clair Drake. Prepared for American Youth Commission, American Council on Education. c1940; rpt. New York: Schocken Books, 1967. 299p.

On Race Relations: Selected Writings. Ed. and intro. by G. Franklin Edwards. Illus. Bibliog. Chicago: Univ. of Chicago Press, 1968. 331p.

Race and Culture Contacts in the Modern World. New York: Knopf, 1957. 338p.

Gaither, Edmund Barry (b. 1944), art historian. Graduate student, Brown Univ., 1966–68; Director, Museum of National Center of Afro-American Artists, Boston, 1968––; Specialist Consultant, Museum of Fine Arts, 1969––; Director, Visual Arts Program, Elma Lewis School of Fine Arts, 1969––; Asst. Prof. of Afro-American Studies, Boston Univ., 1971––.

Reflective Moments: Lois Mailou Jones—Retrospective 1930–1972. Exhibition catalog. Illus. Bibliog. Boston: Museum of National Center of Afro-American Artists and Museum of Fine Arts, 1973. 43p.

Garnet, Henry Highland (1815–1882), abolitionist preacher, essayist. Studied with Alexander Crummell and two other blacks at Noyes Academy, New Canaan, N.H., 1834–35, until irate farmers forced blacks to leave.

The Past and the Present Condition and the Destiny of the Colored Race: A Discourse Delivered at the Fifteenth Anniversary of the Female Benevolent Society of Troy, N.Y., Feb. 14, 1848. 1848 ed.; rpt. Miami, Fla.: Mnemosyne Publishing Co., 1969. 29p.

About Henry Highland Garnet

Ofari, Earl. *Let Your Motto Be Resistance: The Life and Thought of Henry Highland Garnet.* Bibliog. Boston: Beacon Press, 1972. 221p.

Schor, Joel. *Henry Highland Garnet: A Voice of Black Radicalism in the Nineteenth Century.* Bibliog. Westport, Conn.: Greenwood Press, 1977. 250p.

Gates, Henry Louis, Jr. (b. 1950), critic, editor. B.A., Yale Univ., 1973; Assoc. Prof. of English and Afro-American Studies, Director of Black Periodical Fiction Project, Yale Univ.

Ed., *Black Is the Color of the Cosmos: Essays on Afro-American Literature and Culture, 1942–1981,* by Charles T. Davis. Foreword by A. Bartlett Giamatti. Illus. Bibliog. New York: Garland Publishing, 1982. 376p.

Ed., *Black Literature and Literary Theory.* New York and London: Methuen, 1984. 328p.

Ed., *Our Nig; or, Sketches from the Life of a Free Black, In a Two-Story White House, North. Showing that Slavery's Shadows Fall Even There,* by "Our Nig" [Harriet E. Wilson]. Bibliog. New York: Vintage Books, 1983. 140p.

Gilbert, Christopher (b. 1949), poet. M.A., Clark Univ., 1975; clinical psychologist, Boston, Cambridge, Worcester, Mass.

Across the Mutual Landscape. Port Townsend, Wash.: Graywolf Press, 1984. 91p.

Graham, Shirley (see entry for **Du Bois, Shirley Graham**).

Booker T. Washington: Educator of Hand, Head, and Heart. Front. and jacket by Donald W. Lambo. New York: J. Messner, 1955. 192p.

Dr. George Washington Carver, Scientist. With George D. Lipscomb. Illus. by Elton C. Fax. Bibliog. New York: J. Messner, 1944. 248p.

Jean Baptiste Pointe de Sable: Founder of Chicago. New York: J. Messner, 1953. 180p.

Julius K. Nyerere: Teacher of Africa. Bibliog. New York: J. Messner, 1975. 191p.

Paul Robeson: Citizen of the World. Foreword by Carl Van Doren. Illus. Bibliog. c1946; rpt. Westport, Conn.: Negro Universities Press, 1971. 264p.

The Story of Phillis Wheatley. Illus. by Robert Burns. New York: J. Messner, 1949. 176p.

There Once Was a Slave: The Heroic Story of Frederick Douglass. Bibliog. New York: J. Messner, 1947. 310p.

Your Most Humble Servant [Benjamin Banneker]. New York: J. Messner, 1949. 235p.

Grandy, Moses (b. 1786?), author of slave narrative. Born a slave in North Carolina; bought freedom through work in fields and on canal boats; lived in Boston and, in 1843, Portland, Maine; laborer and sailor, bought freedom of wife, son, and grandchild.

Narrative of the Life of Moses Grandy, Late a Slave in the United States of America. "Sold for the benefit of his relations still in slavery." 1844 ed.; rpt. in William Loren Katz, ed., *Five Slave Narratives: A Compendium* (New York: Arno Press, 1968), 46p.

Greene, Lorenzo Johnston (b. 1899), historian. Born in Ansonia, Conn.

The Negro in Colonial New England, 1620–1776. Bibliog. c1942; rpt. Port Washington, N.Y.: Kennikat Press, 1966. 404p.

Gregory, Dick (b. 1932), essayist, autobiographer, speaker. Lives in Plymouth, Mass.

Dick Gregory's Bible Tales, with Commentary. Ed. by James R. McGraw. New York: Stein and Day, 1974. 187p.

Dick Gregory's Natural Diet for Folks Who Eat: Cookin' with Mother Nature! Ed. by James R. McGraw with Alvenia M. Fulton. Bibliog. New York: Harper and Row, 1973. 171p.

Dick Gregory's Political Primer. Ed. by James R. McGraw. Illus. New York: Harper and Row, 1972. 335p.

From the Back of the Bus. Intro. by Hugh M. Hefner. Ed. by Bob Orden. Photos by Jerry Yulsman. New York: Avon Books, 1963. 125p.

Nigger: An Autobiography. With Robert Lipsyte. Illus. New York: Pocket Books, 1965. 209p.

The Shadow That Scares Me. Ed. by James R. McGraw. Garden City, N.Y.: Doubleday, 1968. 213p.

Up from Nigger. Illus. New York: Stein and Day, 1976. 256p.

Gresson, Aaron (b. 1947), social theorist, essayist. Ph.D., Boston College, 1985; Asst. Prof. of Behavioral Studies, Boston Univ., 1977–78; Staff Psychologist, Dr. Solomon Carter Fuller Mental Health Center, 1978–79; Visiting Lecturer in Human Development, Colby College, Maine, 1979–80; Asst. Prof. of Afro-American Studies, Brandeis Univ., 1979–83; Director, Geriatric Services, Dorchester Counseling Center, Boston, 1984––; Adjunct Prof. of Afro-American Studies, Brown Univ., 1985––.

The Dialectics of Betrayal: Sacrifice, Violation, and the Oppressed. Norwood, N.J.: Ablex Publishing Corp., 1982. 150p.

Grimes, William (b. 1784), author of slave narrative. Born a slave in Virginia of slave mother and white father; escaped to New York as stowaway with help of sailors on Boston brig *Casket;* settled in New Haven, Conn., as barber and seller of lottery tickets; bought freedom when threatened by former master with return to slavery in Georgia.

Life of William Grimes, the Runaway Slave, Brought Down to the Present Time. 1855 ed.; rpt. in *Five Black Lives: The Autobiographies of Venture Smith, James Mars, William Grimes, The Rev. G. W. Offley, James L. Smith,* Intro. by Arna Bontemps (Middletown, Conn.: Wesleyan Univ. Press, 1971), 128p.

Grimké, Angelina Weld (1880–1958), playwright, poet. Born and raised in Boston; educated at Girls Latin School, Boston Latin School, and Boston Normal School of Gymnastics.

Rachel: A Play in Three Acts. c1920; rpt. College Park, Md.: McGrath Publishing Co., 1969. 96p.

Hall, Prince (1735?–1807), speaker, author of petitions. A slave in Boston, manumitted in 1770; leatherdresser; founder of black Masonry in America, Master of African Lodge, Boston; active with petitions to legislature for rights of blacks.

A Charge, Delivered to the African Lodge, June 24, 1797, at Menotomy. 1797 ed.; rpt. in Dorothy Porter, *Early Negro Writing 1760–1837* (Boston: Beacon Press, 1971), p. 70–78.

A Charge Delivered to the Brethren of the African Lodge on the 25th of June, 1792, At the Hall of Brother William Smith, in Charlestown. 1792 ed.; rpt. in Dorothy Porter, *Early Negro Writing 1760–1837* (Boston: Beacon Press, 1971), p. 63–69.

About Prince Hall

Wesley, Charles H. *Prince Hall: Life and Legacy.* Illus. Bibliog. 2nd. ed.; United Supreme Council, Southern Jurisdiction, Prince Hall Affiliation, P.O. Box 2959, Washington, D.C. 20013. 1983. 237p.

Hammon, Briton, autobiographer. Slave servant in Marshfield, Mass., left with master's permission on sea voyage from Plymouth in 1747; in England in 1760 accidentally met master, possibly General John Winslow (1703–1774), on ship on which both were returning to Massachusetts.

A Narrative of the Uncommon Sufferings, and Surprising Deliverance of Briton Hammon, a Negro Man,—Servant to General Winslow, of Marshfield, in New England; Who Returned to Boston, After Having Been Absent Almost Thirteen Years. 1760 ed.; rpt. in Dorothy Porter, *Early Negro Writing 1760–1837* (Boston: Beacon Press, 1971), p. 522–528.

A Narrative of the Uncommon Sufferings and Surprizing Deliverance of Briton Hammon, A Negro Man. 1760 ed.; rpt. in Lindsay Patterson, ed., *An Introduction to Black Literature in America: From 1746 to the Present* (Cornwells Heights, Pa.: Publishers Agency, 1976), p. 5–8.

Hare, Maude Cuney (1874–1936), poet, playwright, music historian. Studied at New England Conservatory of Music; lived in Boston area, 1906–36; established Musical Art Studio, Boston, and founded "Little Theatre" movement among blacks; appeared in piano recitals in New England.

Ed., *The Message of the Trees: An Anthology of Leaves and Branches.* Foreword by William Stanley Braithwaite. Illus. Boston: Cornhill Co., 1918. 190p.

Negro Musicians and Their Music. Illus. Bibliog. 1st ed.; Washington, D.C.: Associated Publishers, 1936. 439p.

Negro Musicians and Their Music. Illus. Bibliog. 1936 ed.; rpt. New York: DaCapo Press, 1974. 439p.

Harper, Frances Ellen Watkins (1825–1911), poet, novelist, lecturer. Spoke against slavery in New Bedford, Mass., and Boston; in 1854 engaged by Anti-Slavery Society of Maine as lecturer.

Atlanta Offering: Poems. Illus. 1895 ed.; rpt. Miami, Fla.: Mnemosyne Publishing Co., 1969. 70p.

Idylls of the Bible. Illus. 1901 ed.; rpt. New York: AMS Press, 1975. 64p.

Iola Leroy; or, Shadows Uplifted. Illus. 1893 ed.; rpt. New York: AMS Press, 1971. 282p.

Poems. 1871 ed.; rpt. New York: AMS Press, 1975. 48p.

Poems. c1895; rpt. Freeport, N.Y.: Books for Libraries Press, 1970. 90p.

Poems on Miscellaneous Subjects. 1857 ed.; Chicago: Library Resources, Inc., 1972. 48p. Microbook Library of American Civilization, LAC 40118, Microfilm.

Harper, Michael S. (b. 1938), poet, editor. Israel L. Kapstein Prof. of English, Brown Univ.

Ed., *Chant of Saints: A Gathering of Afro-American Literature, Art, and Scholarship.* With Robert B. Steptoe. Illus. Bibliog. Urbana: Univ. of Illinois Press, 1979. 486p.

Ed., *The Collected Poems of Sterling A. Brown.* New York: Harper and Row, 1980. 257p.

Debridement. Poems. Garden City, N.Y.: Doubleday, 1973. 110p.

History Is Your Own Heartbeat: Poems. Urbana: Univ. of Illinois Press, 1971. 95p.

Images of Kin: New and Selected Poems. Urbana: Univ. of Illinois Press, 1977. 213p.

Nightmare Begins Responsibility. Poems. Urbana: Univ. of Illinois Press, 1974. 97p.

Song: I Want a Witness. Poems. Pittsburgh, Pa.: Univ. of Pittsburgh Press, 1972. 63p.

Hayden, Robert C. (b. 1937), biographer, historian. B.A., 1959, M.Ed., 1961, Boston Univ.; Executive Assistant to Superintendent, Boston Public Schools.

Eight Black American Inventors. Illus. Reading, Mass.: Addison-Wesley, 1972. 142p.

Faith, Culture, and Leadership: A History of the Black Church in Boston. Illus. Boston Branch, NAACP, 451 Massachusetts Ave., Boston, MA 02118. 1983. 56p.

Nine Black American Doctors. With Jacqueline Harris. Illus. Reading, Mass.: Addison-Wesley, 1976. 144p.

Seven Black American Scientists. Illus. Reading, Mass.: Addison-Wesley, 1970. 172p.

Haynes, Lemuel (1753–1833), sermon and letter writer. Born in West Hartford, Conn., of black father and white mother, neither of whom he knew; father said to be of pure African blood; mother of respectable New England family, abandoned him in infancy; at five months, bound out in Middle Granville, Mass., as indentured servant until twenty-one; in 1774 became Minute Man; Congregational minister in Mass., Conn., and Vt.; first black man in America to minister to white congregation.

"The Presence of the Lord": An Unpublished Sermon. Ed. and intro by Richard Newman. Illus. Bibliog. *Bulletin of the Congregational Library*, Vol. 32, No. 1 (Fall 1980), p. 3–13. American Congregational Association, 14 Beacon St., Boston, MA 02108.

Universal Salvation, A Very Ancient Doctrine: With Some Account of the Life and Character of Its Author. A Sermon, Delivered at Rutland, West Parish, Vermont, in the Year 1805. 7th ed.; New York: Printed for Cornelius Davis, 1810. Rpt. in Dorothy Porter, *Early Negro Writing 1760-1837* (Boston: Beacon Press, 1971), p. 448-454.

Heard, William H. (1850-1937), autobiographer. Born a slave in Georgia; Bishop, African Methodist Episcopal Church, First District, Middle Atlantic and New England States, 1920-37.

From Slavery to the Bishopric of the A.M.E. Church: An Autobiography. 1924 ed.; rpt. New York: Arno Press, 1969. 104p.

Henry, George (b. 1819), autobiographer, historian. Escaped from slavery in Virginia, settled in Providence, R.I.; shipped on coastal schooners, led fight for equal rights in public schools.

Life of George Henry; Together with a Brief History of the Colored People in America. Illus. 1894 ed.; rpt. Freeport, N.Y.: Books for Libraries Press, 1971. 123p.

Henson, Josiah (1789-1883), author of slave narrative. Escaped from slavery in Maryland; model for Uncle Tom in *Uncle Tom's Cabin*; visited Harriet Beecher Stowe in her home in Andover, Mass., 1849, and in 1850 at home of her brother Edward Beecher in Boston.

Father Henson's Story of His Own Life. Intro. by Mrs. H. B. Stowe. Illus. 1858 ed.; rpt. Williamstown, Mass.: Corner House Publishers, 1973. 212p.

Father Henson's Story of His Own Life. Intro. by Walter Fisher. Illus. 1858 ed.; rpt. New York: Corinth Books, 1962. 212p.

About Josiah Henson

Bleby, Henry. *Josiah, the Maimed Fugitive: A True Tale.* Illus. 1873 ed.; rpt. Miami, Fla.: Mnemosyne Publishing Co., 1969. 187p.

Hill, Errol (b. 1921), playwright, editor. B.A., 1962, M.A., 1962, D.F.A., 1966, Yale Univ.; Willard Prof. of Drama and Oratory, Dartmouth College.

Strictly Matrimony: A Comedy in One Act. c1971; in Woodie King and Ron Milner, eds., *Black Drama Anthology* (New York: New American Library, 1972), p. 553-574.

Ed., *The Theatre of Black Americans: A Collection of Critical Essays.* Bibliog. 2 vols. Englewood Cliffs, N.J.: Prentice-Hall, 1980. 384p.

GEORGE HENRY

(Reproduced from *Life of George Henry*, 1894)

Hill, Leslie Pinckney (1880–1960), poet, playwright. B.A., 1903, M.A., 1904, Harvard Univ.

The Wings of Oppression. Poems. 1921 ed.; rpt. Freeport, N.Y.: Books for Libraries Press, 1971. 124p.

Hoagland, Everett (b. 1942), poet. M.A., Brown Univ., 1973; Assoc. Prof. of English, Southeastern Massachusetts Univ.

Black Velvet. Illus. Rev. ed.; Detroit: Broadside Press, 1970. 32p.

Scrimshaw: A Celebration of the American Bicentennial. New Bedford, Mass.: Patmos Press, 1976. 31p.

Hopkins, Pauline E. (1859–1930), novelist, short story writer, playwright, editor. Lived most of life in Boston and Cambridge, Mass.; graduated from Girls High School, Boston; stenographer; one of editors of *The Colored American Magazine*, Boston, 1900–1904.

Contending Forces: A Romance Illustrative of Negro Life North and South. Afterword by Gwendolyn Brooks. Illus. by R. Emmet Owen. 1900 ed.; rpt. Carbondale: Southern Illinois Univ. Press, 1978. 411p.

Hagar's Daughter: A Story of Southern Caste Prejudice. By Sarah A. Allen [pseud.]. In *The Colored American Magazine*, Vol. 2, No. 5 (1901), p. 337–352; No. 6, p. 431–445; Vol. 3, No. 1, p. 24–34; No. 2, p. 117–128; No. 3, p. 185–195; No. 4, p. 262–272; No. 5, p. 343–353; No. 6, p. 425–435; Vol. 4, No. 1, p. 23–33; No. 2, p. 113–124; No. 3 (1902), p. 188–200; No. 4, p. 281–291; rpt. New York: Negro Universities Press, 1969.

Of One Blood; or, The Hidden Self. In *The Colored American Magazine*, Vol. 6, No. 1 (1902), p. 29–40; No. 2, p. 101–113; No. 3 (1903), p. 191–200; No. 4, p. 264–272; No. 5, p. 339–348; No. 6, p. 423–432; No. 7, p. 492–501; No. 8, p. 580–586; No. 9, p. 643–647; No. 10, p. 726–731; No. 11, p. 802–807; rpt. New York: Negro Universities Press, 1969.

Winona: A Tale of Negro Life in the South and Southwest. In *The Colored American Magazine*, Vol. 5, No. 1 (1902), p. 29–41; No. 2, p. 97–110; No. 3, p. 177–187; No. 4, p. 257–268; No. 5, p. 348–358; No. 6, p. 422–431; rpt. New York: Negro Universities Press, 1969.

Horton, James Oliver (b. 1943), social historian. Ph.D., Brandeis Univ., 1973.

Black Bostonians: Family Life and Community Struggle in the Antebellum North. With Lois E. Horton. Illus. Bibliog. New York: Holmes and Meier, 1979. 175p.

Huggins, Nathan Irvin (b. 1927), historian. M.A., 1959, Ph.D., 1962, Harvard Univ.; Assoc. Prof. of History, Univ. of Massachusetts, Boston, 1966–70; W. E. B. Du Bois Prof. of History and Afro-American Studies and Director, W. E. B. Du Bois Institute for Afro-American Research, Harvard Univ., 1980—.

Black Odyssey: The Afro-American Ordeal in Slavery. Bibliog. New York: Pantheon Books, 1977. 250p.

Harlem Renaissance. Illus. Bibliog. New York: Oxford Univ. Press, 1971. 343p.

Slave and Citizen: The Life of Frederick Douglass. Bibliog. Boston: Little, Brown, 1980. 194p.

Ed., *Voices from the Harlem Renaissance*. Illus. New York: Oxford Univ. Press, 1976. 438p.

Jackson, Rebecca (1795–1871), religious autobiographer. Visited Providence, R.I., 1835; spoke in churches in New Haven, Middletown, and Hartford, Conn., Springfield and South Wilbraham, Mass., 1840.

Gifts of Power: The Writings of Rebecca Jackson, Black Visionary, Shaker Eldress. Ed. and intro. by Jean McMahon Humez. Bibliog. Amherst: Univ. of Massachusetts Press, 1981. 368p.

Jacobs, Harriet Brent (Brent, Linda [pseud.]) (1815?–1897), author of slave narrative. Born a slave in North Carolina; escaped by ship to North at twenty-seven; spent two years in Boston before 1850 to avoid capture in New York; took refuge twice in New England after passage of Fugitive Slave Act, 1850.

Incidents in the Life of a Slave Girl. Written by Herself. Ed. and intro. by L. Maria Child. 1861 ed.; rpt. Miami, Fla.: Mnemosyne Publishing Co., 1969. 306p.

Jamal, Hakim Abdullah (b. 1931), memoirist. Born and spent early years in Boston.

From the Dead Level: Malcolm X and Me. New York: Random House, 1972. 272p.

Johnson, James Weldon (1871–1938), poet, novelist, autobiographer, editor. In 1926 bought an old farm near Great Barrington, Mass., birthplace of W. E. B. Du Bois, restored barn into cottage for summer home; died on way with his wife from a visit in Point Pleasant, Maine, to Great Barrington when a train struck their car at an unguarded railroad crossing in a blinding rainstorm near Wiscasset, Maine.

Along This Way: The Autobiography of James Weldon Johnson. Illus. New York: Viking Press, 1933. 418p.

The Autobiography of an Ex-Colored Man. A novel. Intro. by Arna Bontemps. 1912 ed.; rpt. New York: Hill and Wang, 1960. 211p.

Black Manhattan. New pref. by Allan H. Spear. c1930; rpt. New York: Atheneum, 1972. 284p.

Ed., *The Book of American Negro Poetry*. Rev. ed., 1931; rpt. New York: Harcourt, Brace and World, 1959. 300p.

Fifty Years and Other Poems. 1917 ed.; rpt. New York: AMS Press, 1975. 92p.

God's Trombones: Seven Negro Sermons in Verse. Drawings by Aaron Douglas, lettering by C. B. Falls. New York: Viking Press, 1927. 56p.

Negro Americans, What Now? c1934; rpt. New York: DaCapo Press, 1973. 103p.

Saint Peter Relates an Incident. Selected poems. 1935 ed.; rpt. New York: AMS Press, 1974. 105p.

About James Weldon Johnson

Bronz, Stephen H. *Roots of Negro Racial Consciousness; the 1920's: Three Harlem Renaissance Authors.* Bibliog. New York: Libra, 1964. 101p.

Felton, Harold W. *James Weldon Johnson.* Illus. by Charles Shaw. New York: Dodd, Mead, 1971. 91p.

Fleming, Robert E. *James Weldon Johnson and Arna Wendell Bontemps: A Reference Guide.* Boston: G. K. Hall, 1978. 149p.

Levy, Eugene. *James Weldon Johnson: Black Leader, Black Voice.* Illus. Bibliog. Chicago: Univ. of Chicago Press, 1973. 380p.

Sterling, Dorothy. *Lift Every Voice: The Lives of Booker T. Washington, W. E. B. Du Bois, Mary Church Terrell, and James Weldon Johnson.* With Benjamin Quarles. Illus. by Ernest Crichlow. Garden City, N.Y.: Doubleday, 1965. 116p.

Jones, Edward Smyth (b. 1881), poet. Attended Harvard Univ.

The Sylvan Cabin: A Centenary Ode on the Birth of Lincoln, and Other Verse. Intro. by William Stanley Braithwaite. Boston: Sherman, French and Co., 1911. 96p.

Jones, Gayl (b. 1949), poet, novelist, short story writer. B.A., Connecticut College, 1971; M.A., Brown Univ., 1973.

Corregidora. New York: Random House, 1975. 185p.

Eva's Man. New York: Random House, 1976. 177p.

Song for Anninho. Detroit: Lotus Press, 1981. 88p.

White Rat: Short Stories. New York: Random House, 1977. 178p.

Jones, Joshua Henry, Jr. (b. 1876), novelist, poet. Attended Brown Univ. and Yale Univ.; served on editorial staffs of newspapers in Providence, R.I., Worcester, Mass., and Boston; secretary to Mayor James Michael Curley, Boston, who appointed him editor of *City Record*; his novel *By Sanction of Law* "Dedicated to my father and the man I revere and most deeply respect next to him, the Honorable James M. Curley, Mayor of Boston."

By Sanction of Law. 1924 ed.; rpt. College Park, Md.: McGrath Publishing Co., 1969. 366p.

Poems of the Four Seas. 1921 ed.; rpt. Freeport, N.Y.: Books for Libraries Press, 1971. 52p.

Jones, Lois Mailou (b. 1905), artist essayist, oral history memoirist. Born and raised in Boston; Diploma, High School of Practical Arts, 1923, School of Museum of Fine Arts, 1927; has spent many summers in Oak Bluffs, Martha's Vineyard.

Interview with Lois Mailou Jones: January 30, 1977, August 6, 1977. Conducted by Theresa Danley. Illus. Cambridge, Mass.: Schlesinger Library, Radcliffe College, 1979. 46p.

Lois Mailou Jones: Peintures, 1937–1951. Illus. Tourcoing, France: Presses Georges Frère, 1952. 125p.

About Lois Mailou Jones

Gaither, Edmund Barry. *Reflective Moments: Lois Mailou Jones—Retrospective 1930–1972.* Exhibition catalog. Illus. Bibliog. Boston: Museum of National Center of Afro-American Artists and Museum of Fine Arts, 1973. 43p.

Jones, Thomas H. (b. 1806?), author of slave narrative. Born a slave in North Carolina; bought wife's freedom, escaped on ship as stowaway with $8 payment to steward, lived with his family in Boston until Fugitive Slave Act, 1850, forced refuge in England.

Experience and Personal Narrative of Uncle Tom Jones: Who Was for Forty Years a Slave. Illus. New York: George C. Holbrook, Publisher and Bookseller, 128 Nassau Street, 1854. 28p. Xerox facsimile.

The Experience of Thomas H. Jones, Who Was a Slave for Forty-Three Years. "Written by a friend, as related to him by Brother Jones." Illus. 1871 ed.; rpt. New York: AMS Press, 1975. 46p.

Jordan, June (b. 1936), poet, essayist, editor, fiction writer. Taught at Yale Univ., 1974–75, and at Connecticut College.

Civil Wars. Essays. Boston: Beacon Press, 1981. 188p.

Dry Victories. Essay. Illus. Bibliog. New York: Holt, Rinehart and Winston, 1972. 80p.

His Own Where. Story. New York: Crowell, 1971. 89p.

Kimako's Story. Illus. by Kay Burford. Boston: Houghton Mifflin, 1981. 42p.

Passion: New Poems, 1977–1980. Pref. by author. Boston: Beacon Press, 1980. 100p.

Some Changes. Poems. New York: Dutton, 1971. 86p.

Ed., *Soulscript: Afro-American Poetry.* Garden City, N.Y.: Doubleday, 1970. 146p.

Things I Do in the Dark: Selected Poetry. New York: Random House, 1977. 203p.

Ed., *The Voice of the Children.* Poems collected with Terri Bush. Illus. New York: Holt, Rinehart and Winston, 1970. 101p.

Who Look at Me. Poem illus. with repro. of 27 paintings. New York: Crowell, 1969. 97p.

Kelley, William Melvin (b. 1937), novelist, short story writer. Attended Harvard Univ., 1956–61.

Dancers on the Shore. Short stories. Garden City, N.Y.: Doubleday, 1964. 201p.

Dem. Garden City, N.Y.: Doubleday, 1967. 210p.

A Different Drummer. 1962 ed.; rpt. Garden City, N.Y.: Anchor Books, 1969. 200p.

A Drop of Patience. 1965 ed.; rpt. Chatham, N.J.: Chatham Bookseller, 1973. 237p.

Dunfords Travels Everywheres. Garden City, N.Y.: Doubleday, 1970. 201p.

Kent, George E. (1920–1982), critic. M.A., 1948, Ph.D., 1953, Boston Univ.; Prof. and Chairman of English and Chairman of Division of Liberal Arts, Quinnipiac College, Conn., 1960–69.

Blackness and the Adventure of Western Culture. Bibliog. Chicago: Third World Press, 1972. 210p.

A Dark and Sudden Beauty: Two Essays in Black American Poetry. With Stephen Henderson. Ed. by Houston A. Baker, Jr. Philadelphia: Afro-American Studies Program, Univ. of Pennsylvania, 1977. 36p.

Kgositsile, Keorapetse William (b. 1938), poet. Attended Univ. of New Hampshire.

For Melba: Poems. Chicago: Third World Press, 1970. 24p.

Khan, Lurey (b. 1927), biographer. Attended Boston College, 1945–46, 1954–55; medical technician, Boston, 1953–65; research assistant in biology, Cambridge, Mass., 1965–78; timekeeper in credit department, retail store, Boston, 1978––.

One Day, Levin. . .He Be Free: William Still and the Underground Railroad. Illus. Bibliog. New York: Dutton, 1972. 231p. '

Kilson, Martin L. (b. 1931), essayist, editor. M.A., 1958, Ph.D., 1959, Harvard Univ.; Prof. of Government, Harvard Univ.

Ed., *The Africa Reader.* Vol. 1, *Colonial Africa.* With Wilfred Cartey. Bibliog. New York: Random House, 1970. 264p.

King, Coretta Scott (b. 1927), memoirist, editor. Attended New England Conservatory of Music, 1951–54.

My Life with Martin Luther King, Jr. Illus. New York: Holt, Rinehart and Winston, 1969. 372p.

The Words of Martin Luther King, Jr. Selected by Coretta Scott King. Illus. Bibliog. New York: Newmarket Press, 1983. 112p.

King, Martin Luther, Jr. (1929–1968), civil rights preacher, essayist. Theological student in Boston, 1951–54; Ph.D., Boston Univ., 1955.

A Martin Luther King Treasury. Photos by Roland Mitchell. Yonkers, N.Y.: Educational Heritage, 1964. 352p.

The Measure of a Man. Illus. c1959; rpt. Philadelphia: Pilgrim Press, 1968. 64p.

Stride Toward Freedom: The Montgomery Story. Illus. New York: Harper, 1958. 230p.

Where Do We Go from Here: Chaos or Community? Bibliog. New York: Harper and Row, 1967. 209p.

Why We Can't Wait. Illus. New York: Harper and Row, 1964. 178p.

The Words of Martin Luther King, Jr. Selected by Coretta Scott King. Illus. Bibliog. New York: Newmarket Press, 1983. 112p.

About Martin Luther King, Jr.

Ansbro, John J. *Martin Luther King, Jr.: The Making of a Mind.* Bibliog. Maryknoll, N.Y.: Orbis Books, 1982. 352p.

Bales, James D. *"The Martin Luther King Story."* Bibliog. Tulsa, Okla.: Christian Crusade Publications, 1967. 224p.

Bennett, Lerone. *What Manner of Man: A Biography of Martin Luther King, Jr.* Intro. by Benjamin E. Mays. Abridged; New York: Pocket Books, 1965. 147p.

Bishop, Jim. *The Days of Martin Luther King, Jr.* Bibliog. New York: Putnam, 1971. 516p.

Boutelle, Paul (and others). *Murder in Memphis: Martin Luther King, Jr., and the Future of the Black Liberation Struggle.* Illus. New York: Merit Publishers, 1968. 15p.

Clark, Kenneth B. *The Negro Protest: James Baldwin, Malcolm X, Martin Luther King Talk with Kenneth B. Clark.* Boston: Beacon Press, 1963. 56p.

Davis, Lenwood G. *I Have a Dream: The Life and Times of Martin Luther King, Jr.* Bibliog. 1969 ed.; rpt. Westport, Conn.: Negro Universities Press, 1977. 303p.

Frank, Gerold. *An American Death: The True Story of the Assassination of Dr. Martin Luther King, Jr., and the Greatest Manhunt of Our Time.* Illus. Garden City, N.Y.: Doubleday, 1972. 467p.

Huie, William Bradford. *He Slew the Dreamer: My Search, with James Earl Ray, for the Truth about the Murder of Martin Luther King.* New York: Delacorte Press, 1970. 212p.

King, Coretta Scott. *My Life with Martin Luther King, Jr.* Illus. New York: Holt, Rinehart and Winston, 1969. 372p.

Lewis, David Levering. *King: A Biography.* Bibliog. Urbana: Univ. of Illinois Press, 1978. 468p.

Lomax, Louis E. *To Kill a Black Man.* Los Angeles: Holloway House Publishing Co., 1968. 256p.

Lyght, Ernest Shaw. *The Religious and Philosophical Foundations in the Thought of Martin Luther King, Jr.* Bibliog. New York: Vantage Press, 1972. 96p.

Miller, William Robert. *Martin Luther King, Jr.: His Life, Martyrdom, and Meaning for the World.* Illus. Bibliog. New York: Weybright and Talley, 1968. 319p.

Oates, Stephen B. *Let the Trumpet Sound: The Life of Martin Luther King, Jr.* Illus. Bibliog. New York: Harper and Row, 1982. 560p.

Reddick, Lawrence Dunbar. *Crusader Without Violence: A Biography of Martin Luther King, Jr.* Illus. New York: Harper, 1959. 243p.

Time-Life Books. *I Have a Dream: The Story of Martin Luther King in Text and Pictures.* New York: Time-Life Books, 1968. 96p.

Walton, Hanes. *The Political Philosophy of Martin Luther King, Jr.* Intro. by Samuel DuBois Cook. Bibliog. Westport, Conn.: Greenwood Publishing Corp., 1971. 137p.

King, Mel (b. 1928), social historian. Born and has lived most of life in Boston; Diploma, Boston Technical High School; M.Ed., State Teachers College, Boston; social worker and community activist; State Representative, 1973–81; Director, Community Fellows Program, Massachusetts Institute of Technology.

Chain of Change: Struggles for Black Community Development. Bibliog. Boston: South End Press, 1981. 304p.

Kountze, Mabe (b. 1910), journalist. Born and has lived entire life in West Medford, Mass.; journalist with *Boston Chronicle*, 1930–40, *Boston Guardian*, 1940–57.

Fifty Sports Years Along Memory Lane: A Newspaperman's Research, Views, Comment, and Career; Story of United States, Hometown, National and International Afro-American Sports History. Illus. Bibliog. Medford, Mass.: Mystic Valley Press, 1979. 185p.

This Is Your Heritage: A Newspaperman's Research, Sketches, Views, and Comment; United States, Hometown, and World History. Illus. Medford, Mass.: Pothier Bros., 1968. 592p.

Lacy, Leslie Alexander (b. 1937), biographer, autobiographer. Attended Tufts Univ. for two years.

Cheer the Lonesome Traveler: The Life of W. E. B. Du Bois. Illus. by James Barkley, and with photos. Bibliog. New York: Dial Press, 1970. 183p.

The Rise and Fall of a Proper Negro: An Autobiography. New York: Macmillan, 1970. 244p.

Lane, Lunsford (b. 1803), author of slave narrative. Born a slave in North Carolina; paid owner for manumission, 1835; solicited $1080 at houses, businesses, and churches in Boston, 1842, to buy family's freedom; settled in Boston, travelled in New England as antislavery lecturer until about 1856, when left for Oberlin, Ohio.

The Narrative of Lunsford Lane, Formerly of Raleigh, N.C.: Embracing an account of his early life, the redemption by purchase of himself and family from slavery, and his banishment from the place of his birth for the crime of wearing a colored skin. 1842 ed.; rpt. in William Loren Katz, ed., *Five Slave Narratives: A Compendium* (New York: Arno Press, 1968), 56p.

About Lunsford Lane

Hawkins, William G. *Lunsford Lane; Another Helper from North Carolina.* Illus. 1863 ed.; rpt. Miami, Fla.: Mnemosyne Publishing Co., 1969. 305p.

Lee, Andrea (b. 1953), novelist. Attended Radcliffe College, 1977–82.

Sarah Phillips. New York: Random House, 1984. 224p.

Lester, Julius (b. 1939), essayist, memoirist, short story writer, editor. Has lived on Martha's Vineyard and in Cambridge, Mass.; teaches in Afro-American Studies and Judaic Studies, Univ. of Massachusetts, Amherst.

All Is Well. New York: Morrow, 1976. 319p.

Long Journey Home: Stories from Black History. New York: Dial Press, 1972. 147p.

Look Out, Whitey! Black Power's Gon' Get your Mama! Bibliog. New York: Dial Press, 1968. 152p.

Search for the New Land: History as Subjective Experience. New York: Dial Press, 1969. 195p.

Ed., *The Seventh Son: The Thought and Writings of W. E. B. Du Bois.* 2 vols. Bibliog. New York: Random House, 1971. 767p.

This Strange New Feeling. Stories. New York: Dial Press, 1982. 149p.

Ed., *To Be a Slave.* Illus. by Tom Feelings. Bibliog. New York: Dial Press, 1968. 160p.

Two Love Stories. New York: Dial Press, 1972. 180p.

Levy, Lyn A. (b. 1946), poet, critic. Born in Boston, attended Northeastern Univ.

Singing Sadness Happy: Poems by Lyn. Detroit: Broadside Press, 1972. 32p.

Lincoln, C. Eric (b. 1924), social historian, essayist, editor. M.Ed., 1960, Ph.D., 1960, Boston Univ.; taught at Dartmouth College, 1962–63.

Ed., *The Black Experience in Religion.* Bibliog. Garden City, N.Y.: Anchor Press, 1974. 369p.

The Black Muslims in America. Foreword by Gordon Allport. Bibliog. Boston: Beacon Press, 1961. 276p.

Ed., *Is Anybody Listening to Black America?* Bibliog. New York: Seabury Press, 1968. 280p.

My Face Is Black. Bibliog. Boston: Beacon Press, 1964. 137p.

The Negro Pilgrimage in America: The Coming of Age of the Black Americans. Illus. New York: Bantam Books, 1969. 209p.

Ed., *A Pictorial History of the Negro in America*, by Langston Hughes and Milton Meltzer. Bibliog. 3rd rev. ed. by C. Eric Lincoln and Milton Meltzer; New York: Crown Publishers, 1968. 380p.

Sounds of the Struggle: Persons and Perspectives in Civil Rights. Bibliog. New York: Morrow, 1967. 252p.

Little, Malcolm (see entry for **Malcolm X**).

Locke, Alain LeRoy (1886–1954), cultural essayist, historian, editor. B.A., 1907, Ph.D., 1918, Harvard Univ.

The Critical Temper of Alain Locke: A Selection of His Essays on Art and Culture. Ed. by Jeffrey C. Stewart. Illus. Bibliog. New York: Garland Publishing, 1983. 491p.

Ed., *A Decade of Negro Self-Expression*. Foreword by Howard W. Odum. Bibliog. 1928 ed.; Xerox facsimile, Ann Arbor, Mich.: University Microfilms, 1975. 20p.

The Negro and His Music and *Negro Art: Past and Present*. 1936 ed.; rpt. New York: Arno Press, 1969. 142p., 122p.

Ed., *The New Negro: An Interpretation*. Illus. Bibliog. 1925 ed.; rpt. New York: Arno Press, 1968. 446p.

Ed., *The New Negro: An Interpretation*. New intro. by Allan H. Spear. Illus. Bibliog. 1925 ed.; rpt. New York: Johnson Reprint Corp., 1968. 446p.

Ed., *Plays of Negro Life: A Source-Book of Native American Drama*. With Montgomery Gregory. Decorations and illus. by Aaron Douglas. Bibliog. New York and London: Harper and Brothers, 1927. 430p.

Ed., *When Peoples Meet: A Study in Race and Culture Contacts*. With Bernhard J. Stern. Rev. ed.; New York: Hinds, Hayden and Eldredge, 1946. 825p.

About Alain LeRoy Locke

Linnemann, Russell J., ed. *Alain Locke: Reflections on a Modern Renaissance Man*. Bibliog. Baton Rouge: Louisiana State Univ. Press, 1982. 146p.

Logan, Rayford W. (1897–1982), historian. B.A., 1917, M.A., 1929, Williams College; M.A., 1932, Ph.D., 1936, Harvard Univ.

The Betrayal of the Negro: From Rutherford B. Hayes to Woodrow Wilson. Bibliog. Orig. pub. as *The Negro In American Life and Thought: The Nadir, 1877–1901*. New enl. ed.; New York: Collier Books, 1965. 447p.

Ed., *Dictionary of American Negro Biography*. With Michael R. Winston. New York: Norton, 1982. 680p.

Four Took Freedom: The Lives of Harriet Tubman, Frederick Douglass, Robert Smalls, and Blanche K. Bruce. With Philip Sterling. Illus. by Charles White. Garden City, N.Y.: Doubleday, 1967. 116p.

The Negro in American Life and Thought: The Nadir, 1877–1901. Bibliog. New York: Dial Press, 1954. 380p.

The Negro in the United States: A Brief History. Bibliog. Princeton, N.J.: D. Van Nostrand Co., 1957. 191p.

Ed., *W. E. B. Du Bois: A Profile*. New York: Hill and Wang, 1971. 324p.

Ed., *What the Negro Wants*, by Mary McLeod Bethune and others. c1944; rpt. New York: Agathon Press, 1969. 352p.

Malcolm X (Malcolm Little) (1925–1965), autobiographer, speaker. Lived on Waumbeck St., Roxbury section of Boston, 1940–41; led burglary gang which operated from apartment in Harvard Square, Cambridge, 1945–46; sentenced in 1946 to ten years in prison; served in Charlestown, Concord, and Norfolk, Mass., state prisons until parole in 1952; became Muslim minister, spoke in Boston, 1962, and at Harvard Univ., 1961 and 1964.

The Autobiography of Malcolm X. With assistance of and epilogue by Alex Haley. Intro. by M. S. Handler. Illus. New York: Grove Press, 1965. 455p.

The End of White World Supremacy: Four Speeches. Ed. and intro. by Benjamin Goodman. New York: Merlin House; distributed by Monthly Review Press, 1971. 148p.

Malcolm X on Afro-American History. Expanded and illus. ed.; New York: Pathfinder Press, 1970. 74p.

The Speeches of Malcolm X at Harvard. Ed. and intro. by Archie Epps. Bibliog. New York: Morrow, 1968. 191p.

About Malcolm X

Baldwin, James. *One Day, When I Was Lost: A Scenario.* Based on Alex Haley's *The Autobiography of Malcolm X.* Illus. New York: Dial Press, 1973. 280p.

Breitman, George. *The Assassination of Malcolm X: Unanswered Questions.* Also *The Trial*, by Herman Porter. Illus. New York: Merit Publishers, 1969. 31p.

Clark, Kenneth B. *The Negro Protest: James Baldwin, Malcolm X, Martin Luther King Talk with Kenneth B. Clark.* Boston: Beacon Press, 1963. 56p.

Clarke, John Henrik, ed. *Malcolm X: The Man and His Times.* With A. Peter Bailey and Earl Grant. New York: Macmillan, 1969. 360p.

Cleage, Albert B. and **George Breitman.** *Myths About Malcolm X: Two Views.* New York: Merit Publishers, 1968. 30p.

Goldman, Peter. *The Death and Life of Malcolm X.* Illus. New York: Harper and Row, 1973. 438p.

Jamal, Hakim A. *From the Dead Level: Malcolm X and Me.* New York: Random House, 1972. 272p.

Lomax, Louis A. *To Kill a Black Man.* Los Angeles: Holloway House Publishing Co., 1968. 256p.

Randall, Dudley, ed. *For Malcolm: Poems on the Life and Death of Malcolm X.* With Margaret Burroughs. Pref. and eulogy by Ossie Davis. Illus. Bibliog. Detroit: Broadside Press, 1969. 127p.

Manning, Kenneth R. (b. 1947), biographer. B.A., 1970, M.A., 1971, Ph.D., 1974, Harvard Univ.; Assoc. Prof. of History of Science and Acting Head, Writing Program, Dept. of Humanities, Massachusetts Institute of Technology.

Black Apollo of Science: The Life of Ernest Everett Just. Illus. Bibliog. New York: Oxford Univ. Press, 1983. 397p.

Marrant, John (1755–1791), autobiographer, preacher. Missionary to Indians; joined African Lodge of Free and Accepted Masons, Boston, 1789; became Chaplain at request of Prince Hall, Grand Master; delivered sermon to lodge on Festival of St. John the Baptist, 1789, probably in Faneuil Hall; returned to London, 1790.

A Narrative of the Lord's Wonderful Dealings with John Marrant, a Black (Now gone to preach the Gospel in Nova Scotia), Born in New York, in North America. 7th ed., 1802; rpt. in Dorothy Porter, *Early Negro Writing 1760–1837* (Boston: Beacon Press, 1971), p. 427–447.

"The Conversion of a Young Musician," from *A Narrative of the Lord's Wonderful Dealings with J. Marrant, a Black.* 1785 ed.; rpt. in Lindsay Patterson, ed., *An Introduction to Black Literature in America: From 1746 to the Present* (Cornwells Heights, Pa.: Publishers Agency, 1976), p. 19–21.

Mars, James (b. 1790), autobiographer. Born the slave of a minister in North Canaan, Conn.; sold at eight to a farmer in Norfolk, Conn., until twenty-five; then lived in Hartford and in Pittsfield, Mass.

Life of James Mars, a Slave Born and Sold in Connecticut. Written by Himself. 1864 ed.; rpt. in *Five Black Lives: The Autobiographies of Venture Smith, James Mars, William Grimes, The Rev. G. W. Offley, James L. Smith,* Intro. by Arna Bontemps (Middletown, Conn.: Wesleyan Univ. Press, 1971), p. 35–58. 8th ed., 1869; rpt. Miami, Fla.: Mnemosyne Publishing Co., 1969. 38p.

Martin, Tony (b. 1942), historian, biographer. Prof. of Black Studies, Wellesley College.

Literary Garveyism: Garvey, Black Arts, and the Harlem Renaissance. Illus. Bibliog. Dover, Mass.: Majority Press, 1983. 204p.

Marcus Garvey, Hero: A First Biography. Illus. Bibliog. Dover, Mass.: Majority Press, 1983. 179p.

Ed., *The Poetical Works of Marcus Garvey.* Bibliog. Dover, Mass.: Majority Press, 1983. 123p.

Race First: The Ideological and Organizational Struggles of Marcus Garvey and the Universal Negro Improvement Association. Bibliog. Westport, Conn.: Greenwood Press, 1976. 421p.

Mason, Isaac (b. 1822), author of slave narrative. Escaped with wife from slavery in Maryland through Underground Railroad to Boston, settled in Worcester, Mass.

Life of Isaac Mason as a Slave. Illus. 1893 ed.; rpt. Miami, Fla.: Mnemosyne Publishing Co., 1969. 74p.

Mays, Benjamin E. (1895–1984), essayist, autobiographer. B.A., Bates College, 1920.

Born to Rebel: An Autobiography. Illus. New York: Scribner's, 1971. 380p.

The Negro's God as Reflected in His Literature. New pref. by Vincent Harding. Illus. c1938; rpt. New York: Atheneum, 1969. 269p.

McClaurin, Irma (b. 1952), poet. M.F.A., Univ. of Massachusetts, Amherst, 1976; Visiting Lecturer, Simon's Rock Early College, Great Barrington, 1974; Asst. Director of Admissions, Mt. Holyoke College, 1975–77; Poet-in-the-Schools, Massachusetts Council for the Arts, Pittsfield, 1976; Asst. Director of Transfer Admissions, 1977–81, Assoc. Director, 1981–83, Asst. Dean, College of Arts and Sciences, 1983––, Univ. of Massachusetts.

Black Chicago. New York: Rannick Amuru Press, 1971. 30p.

Song in the Night. Amherst, Mass.: Pearl Press, 1974. 30p. Distributed by the Author, 94 Pondview Drive, Amherst, MA 01002.

McClellan, George Marion (1860–1934), poet, short story writer. B.D., Hartford, Conn., Theological Seminary, 1886.

Old Greenbottom Inn, and Other Stories. 1906 ed.; rpt. New York: AMS Press, 1975. 210p.

The Path of Dreams. 1916 ed.; Freeport, N.Y.: Books for Libraries Press, 1971. 206p.

Poems. 1895 ed.; rpt. Freeport, N.Y.: Books for Libraries Press, 1970. 145p.

McCluskey, John A. (b. 1944), novelist. B.A., Harvard Univ., 1966.

Look What They Done to My Song. New York: Random House, 1974. 251p.

Mr. America's Last Season Blues. Baton Rouge: Louisiana State Univ. Press, 1983. 243p.

McKay, Claude (1890–1948), poet, novelist, short story writer, autobiographer, social essayist. Early in career, worked short time as kitchen worker in New England hotels.

Banana Bottom. c1933; rpt. Chatham, N.J.: Chatham Bookseller, 1970. 317p.

Banjo: A Story Without a Plot. 1929 ed.; rpt. New York: Harcourt Brace, 1957. 326p.

The Dialect Poetry of Claude McKay. Contains *Songs of Jamaica* and *Constab Ballads.* Pref. by Wayne Cooper. Illus. 1912 ed.; rpt. Freeport, N.Y.: Books for Libraries Press, 1972. 140p., 94p.

Gingertown. Stories. 1932 ed.; rpt. Freeport, N.Y.: Books for Libraries Press, 1972. 274p.

Harlem: Negro Metropolis. Illus. with photos. c1940; rpt. New York: Harcourt, Brace, 1968. 262p.

Home to Harlem. c1928; rpt. New York: Pocket Books, 1965. 180p.

A Long Way from Home. Autobiography. Intro. by St. Clair Drake. c1937; rpt. New York: Harcourt, Brace and World, 1970. 354p.

The Negroes in America. Ed. by Alan L. McLeod. Transl. from the Russian by Robert J. Winter. 1923 ed.; 1st English ed., Port Washington, N.Y.: Kennikat Press, 1979. 97p.

The Passion of Claude McKay: Selected Poetry and Prose, 1912-1948. Ed. and intro. by Wayne F. Cooper. Illus. Bibliog. New York: Schocken Books, 1973. 363p.

Selected Poems. Biog. note by Max Eastman. New York: Harcourt, Brace and World, 1953. 112p.

Songs of Jamaica. Intro. by Walter Jekyll. Illus. 1912 ed.; rpt. Miami, Fla.: Mnemosyne Publishing Co., 1969. 140p.

About Claude McKay

Bronz, Stephen H. *Roots of Negro Racial Consciousness; the 1920's: Three Harlem Renaissance Authors.* Bibliog. New York: Libra, 1964. 101p.

Giles, James R. *Claude McKay.* Bibliog. Boston: Twayne Publishers, 1976. 170p.

McKay, Nellie Y. (b. 1946), biographer, critic. M.A., 1971, Ph.D., 1977, Harvard Univ.; Instructor in English, 1971-73, Asst. Prof., 1973-78, Simmons College, Boston; was Adjunct Prof. of Afro-American Literature, Northeastern Univ.

Jean Toomer, Artist: A Study of His Literary Life and Work, 1894-1936. Illus. Bibliog. Chapel Hill: Univ. of North Carolina Press, 1984. 262p.

McPherson, James Alan (b. 1943), short story writer. LL.B., Harvard Law School, 1968.

Elbow Room. Boston: Little, Brown, 1977. 241p.

Hue and Cry. Boston: Little, Brown, 1969. 275p.

Menkiti, Ifeanyi (b. 1940), poet. Ph.D., Harvard Univ., 1974; Assoc. Prof. of Philosophy, Wellesley College.

Affirmations. Chicago: Third World Press, 1971. 24p.

The Jubilation of Falling Bodies. Illus. by Karyl Klopp. Cambridge, Mass.: Pomegranate Press, 1978. 30p.

Morrow, E. Frederic (b. 1909), memoirist. B.A., Bowdoin College, 1930.

Black Man in the White House: A Diary of the Eisenhower Years. By the Administrative Officer for Special Projects, The White House, 1955–1961. New York: Macfadden-Bartell, 1963. 222p.

Moses, Wilson Jeremiah (b. 1942), cultural historian, essayist, poet. Ph.D., Brown Univ., 1975; Assoc. Prof. of American Civilization and Afro-American Studies, Brown Univ.

Black Messiahs and Uncle Toms: Social and Literary Manipulations of a Religious Myth. Bibliog. University Park: Pennsylvania State Univ. Press, 1982. 278p.

Murray, Pauli (b. 1910), poet, memoirist. J.S.D., Yale Law School, 1965; was Prof. of American Studies, Brandeis Univ.

Dark Testament and Other Poems. Norwalk, Conn.: Silvermine, 1970. 106p.

Proud Shoes: The Story of an American Family. New York: Harper, 1956. 276p.

Naylor, Gloria (b. 1950), novelist. M.A. in Afro-American Studies, Yale Univ., 1983.

Linden Hills. New York: Ticknor and Fields, 1985. 304p.

The Women of Brewster Place. New York: Viking Press, 1982. 192p.

Neal, Larry (b. 1937), poet, editor. Writer-in-Residence, Wesleyan Univ., Conn., 1969– 70; Fellow, Yale Univ., 1971–75.

Ed., *Black Fire: An Anthology of Afro-American Writing.* With LeRoi Jones. Illus. New York: Morrow, 1968. 670p.

Hoodoo Hollerin' Bebop Ghosts. Poems. Washington, D.C.: Howard Univ. Press, 1974. 87p.

Nell, William Cooper (1816–1874), historian, journalist. Born and lived most of life in Boston; long active abolitionist with William Lloyd Garrison in publication of *The Liberator*; in 1850 helped form Committee of Vigilance to undermine Fugitive Slave Act; active in Underground Railroad; led effort to end segregated schools in Boston with Massachusetts legislative act of 1855.

The Colored Patriots of the American Revolution; with Sketches of Several Distinguished Colored Persons: To Which Is Added a Brief Survey of the Condition and Prospects of Colored Americans. Intro. by Harriet Beecher Stowe. 1855 ed.; rpt. New York: Arno Press, 1968. 396p.

Services of Colored Americans in the Wars of 1776 and 1812. 1851 ed.; rpt. New York: AMS Press, 1976. 24p.

Newton, Alexander Herritage (b. 1837), autobiographer, preacher, essayist. Did abolitionist work in Connecticut, served with Conn. regiment in Civil War, was African Methodist Episcopal minister in New England.

Out of the Briars: An Autobiography and Sketch of the Twenty-Ninth Regiment, Connecticut Volunteers. Intro. by J. P. Sampson. Illus. 1910 ed.; rpt. Miami, Fla.: Mnemosyne Publishing Co., 1969. 269p.

Nichols, Charles H. (b. 1919), essayist, editor. Ph.D., Brown Univ., 1948; Prof. of English, Brown Univ.

Ed., *Arna Bontemps-Langston Hughes Letters, 1925–1967.* Illus. Bibliog. New York: Dodd, Mead, 1980. 529p.

Ed., *Black Men in Chains: Narratives by Escaped Slaves.* Bibliog. New York: L. Hill, 1972. 319p.

Many Thousand Gone: The Ex-Slaves' Account of Their Bondage and Freedom. Leiden, Holland: E. J. Brill, 1963. 229p.

Offley, G.W. (b. 1808), author of slave narrative. Born a slave in Maryland; bought by his father, a free black; freed at twenty-one, settled in Hartford, Conn., 1835; became Methodist Episcopal minister.

A Narrative of the Life and Labors of the Rev. G. W. Offley, A Colored Man, and Local Preacher. 1860 ed.; rpt. in *Five Black Lives: The Autobiographies of Venture Smith, James Mars, William Grimes, The Rev. G. W. Offley, James L. Smith,* Intro. by Arna Bontemps (Middletown, Conn.: Wesleyan Univ. Press, 1971), p. 129–137.

Ovington, Mary White (1865–1951), essayist, playwright, biographer, memoirist, writer of fiction for young people. Spent childhood summers in Chesterfield, Mass.; attended Radcliffe College, 1891–93; had summer home in Great Barrington; died in Newton.

The Awakening: A Play. 1923 ed.; rpt. Freeport, N.Y.: Books for Libraries Press, 1972. 64p.

Half a Man: The Status of the Negro in New York. Intro. by Charles Flint Kellogg. Bibliog. 1911 ed.; rpt. New York: Hill and Wang, 1969. 128p.

Hazel. A novel. Illus. by Harry Roseland. 1913 ed.; rpt. Freeport, N.Y.: Books for Libraries Press, 1972. 162p.

The Shadow. A novel. 1920 ed.; rpt. Freeport, N.Y.: Books for Libraries Press, 1972. 352p.

The Walls Came Tumbling Down. Memoirs. With new intro. Bibliog. 1947 ed.; rpt. New York: Arno Press, 1969. 307p.

Patterson, Lindsay (b. 1937), editor, critic. Has had three fellowships at MacDowell Colony, Peterborough, N.H.

Ed., *The Afro-American in Music and Art.* Illus. Bibliog. International Library of Afro-American Life and History, Vol. 5. Earlier ed. pub. under title *The Negro in Music and Art.* Rev. ed.; Cornwells Heights, Pa.: Publishers Agency, 1976. 304p.

Ed., *Anthology of the Afro-American in the Theatre: A Critical Approach.* Illus. Bibliog. International Library of Afro-American Life and History, Vol. 3. Earlier ed. pub. under title *Anthology of the American Negro in the Theatre: A Critical Approach.* Rev. ed.; Cornwells Heights, Pa.: Publishers Agency, 1976. 306p.

Ed., *Black Films and Film-Makers: A Comprehensive Anthology from Stereotype to Superhero.* Illus. Bibliog. New York: Dodd, Mead, 1975. 298p.

Ed., *Black Theater: A 20th Century Collection of the Work of Its Best Playwrights.* New York: Dodd, Mead, 1971. 493p.

Ed., *An Introduction to Black Literature in America: From 1746 to the Present.* Illus. Bibliog. International Library of Afro-American Life and History, Vol. 10. Rev. ed.; Cornwells Heights, Pa.: Publishers Agency, 1976. 302p.

Ed., *A Rock Against the Wind: Black Love Poems; An Anthology.* New York: Dodd, Mead, 1973. 172p.

Patterson, Orlando (b. 1940), social historian, novelist. Prof. of Sociology, Harvard Univ.

Ethnic Chauvinism: The Reactionary Impulse. New York: Stein and Day, 1977. 347p.

Slavery and Social Death: A Comparative Study. Bibliog. Cambridge, Mass.: Harvard Univ. Press, 1982. 511p.

Pennington, James W.C. (1809–1870), historian, author of slave narrative. Fugitive slave from Maryland; studied theology in New Haven, Conn.; first pastorate at Colored Congregational Church, Talcott St., Hartford, 1841.

The Fugitive Blacksmith; or, Events in the History of James W.C. Pennington, Pastor of a Presbyterian Church, New York, Formerly a Slave in the State of Maryland, United States. 1849 ed.; rpt. in William Loren Katz, ed., *Five Slave Narratives: A Compendium* (New York: Arno Press, 1968), 84p.; Arna Bontemps, ed., *Great Slave Narratives* (Boston: Beacon Press, 1969), p. 193–267. 3rd ed., 1850; rpt. Westport, Conn.: Negro Universities Press, 1971. 84p.

A Text Book of the Origin and History, &c. &c. of the Colored People. 1841 ed.; Negro History Press, P.O. Box 5129, Detroit, MI 48236. 1969. 96p.

Peterson, Lewis (b. 1922), playwright. Born and raised in Hartford, Conn.; attended School of Drama, Yale Univ.

Take a Giant Step. c1954; in Darwin T. Turner, ed., *Black Drama in America: An Anthology* (Greenwich, Conn.: Fawcett Publications, 1971), p. 297–375; James V. Hatch, editor, and Ted Shine, consultant, *Black Theater U.S.A.: Forty-Five Plays by Black Americans, 1847–1974* (New York: Free Press, 1974), p. 547–584.

Petry, Ann (b. 1911), novelist, short story writer, writer of books for young people. Born and has lived most of life in Old Saybrook, Conn.; graduate, Connecticut College of Pharmacy, 1931; registered pharmacist, Old Saybrook and Old Lyme, 1931–38.

Country Place. 1947 ed.; rpt. Chatham, N.J.: Chatham Bookseller, 1971. 266p.

The Drugstore Cat. Illus. by Susanne Saba. 1949 ed.; Xerox facsimile, Ann Arbor, Mich.: University Microfilms, 1974. 87p.

Harriet Tubman: Conductor on the Underground Railroad. New York: Crowell, 1955. 247p.

Legends of the Saints. Illus. by Anne Rockwell. New York: Crowell, 1970. 47p.

Miss Muriel and Other Stories. Boston: Houghton Mifflin, 1971. 305p.

The Narrows. Boston: Houghton Mifflin, 1953. 428p.

The Street. c1945; rpt. New York: Pyramid Books, 1972. 270p.

Tituba of Salem Village. New York: Crowell, 1964. 254p.

Ann Petry

Pharr, Robert Deane (b. 1916), novelist. Raised in New Haven, Conn.; graduate, New Haven High School.

The Book of Numbers. Garden City, N.Y.: Doubleday, 1969. 374p.

Giveadamn Brown. Garden City, N.Y.: Doubleday, 1978. 212p.

S.R.O. Garden City, N.Y.: Doubleday, 1971. 569p.

Pickens, William (1881–1954), essayist, biographer, autobiographer. B.A., Yale Univ., 1904.

American Aesop: Negro and Other Humor. 1926 ed.; rpt. New York: AMS Press, 1969. 183p.

The New Negro: His Political, Civil, and Mental Status; and Related Essays. 1916 ed.; rpt. New York: AMS Press, 1969. 239p.

The Vengeance of the Gods; and Three Other Stories of Real American Color Line Life. Intro. by Bishop John Hurst. 1922 ed.; rpt. Freeport, N.Y.: Books for Libraries Press, 1972. 125p.

Pitcher, Oliver (b. 1924), playwright, poet. Born in Massachusetts.

The One: A Play. c1971; in Woodie King and Ron Milner, eds., *Black Drama Anthology* (New York: New American Library, 1972), p. 243–251.

Poindexter, Hildrus Augustus (b. 1901), autobiographer. Attended Dartmouth College Medical School; M.D., Harvard Medical School, 1929.

My World of Reality: An Autobiography. Illus. Detroit: Balamp Pub., 1973. 342p.

Powell, Adam Clayton, Jr. (1908–1972), social historian. Born in New Haven, Conn.

Marching Blacks: An Interpretive History of the Rise of the Black Common Man. Bibliog. 1st ed.; New York: Dial Press, 1945. 218p.

Marching Blacks. Rev. ed.; New York: Dial Press, 1973. 216p.

About Adam Clayton Powell, Jr.

Dionisopoulos, P. Allan. *Rebellion, Racism, and Representation: The Adam Clayton Powell Case and Its Antecedents.* Bibliog. Dekalb: Northern Illinois Univ. Press, 1970. 175p.

Jacobs, Andy. *The Powell Affair: Freedom Minus One.* Indianapolis, Ind.: Bobbs-Merrill, 1973. 256p.

Powell, Adam Clayton, Sr. (1865–1953), autobiographer, essayist. Attended Yale Divinity School, 1895–96; pastor, Immanuel Baptist Church, New Haven, Conn., 1893–1908.

Against the Tide: An Autobiography. Illus. 1938 ed.; rpt. New York: Arno Press, 1980. 327p.

Proctor, Henry Hugh (1868–1933), autobiographer. B.D., Yale Divinity School, 1894.

Between Black and White: Autobiographical Sketches. Illus. 1925 ed.; rpt. Freeport, N.Y.: Books for Libraries Press, 1971. 189p.

Quarles, Benjamin (b. 1904), historian. Born in Boston, educated in public schools there.

Black Abolitionists. Bibliog. New York: Oxford Univ. Press, 1969. 310p.

Black History's Antebellum Origins. Bibliog. Worcester, Mass.: American Antiquarian Society, 1979. 33p.

Ed., *Blacks on John Brown.* Bibliog. Urbana: Univ. of Illinois Press, 1972. 164p.

Ed., *Frederick Douglass.* Bibliog. Englewood Cliffs, N.J.: Prentice-Hall, 1968. 184p.

Frederick Douglass. A biography. New pref. by James M. McPherson. Illus. Bibliog. 1948 ed.; rpt. New York: Atheneum, 1969. 378p.

Lift Every Voice: The Lives of Booker T. Washington, W. E. B. Du Bois, Mary Church Terrell, and James Weldon Johnson. With Dorothy Sterling. Illus. by Ernest Crichlow. Garden City, N.Y.: Doubleday, 1965. 116p.

Lincoln and the Negro. Bibliog. New York: Oxford Univ. Press, 1962. 275p.

The Negro in the American Revolution. Bibliog. Chapel Hill: Univ. of North Carolina Press, 1961. 231p.

The Negro in the Civil War. Illus. Bibliog. 1953 ed.; rpt. Boston: Little, Brown, 1969. 379p.

The Negro in the Making of America. Bibliog. Rev. ed.; New York: Collier Books, 1969. 318p.

Redding, J. Saunders (b. 1906), critic, historian, novelist. Ph.B., 1928, M.A., 1932, Brown Univ.; Visiting Prof., Brown Univ., 1949–50.

Ed., *Cavalcade: Negro American Writing from 1760 to the Present.* With Arthur P. Davis. Illus. Bibliog. Boston: Houghton Mifflin, 1971. 905p.

No Day of Triumph. Intro. by Richard Wright. c1942; rpt. New York: Harper and Row, 1968. 342p.

They Came in Chains: Americans from Africa. Bibliog. Philadelphia: Lippincott, 1950. 320p.

To Make a Poet Black. Bibliog. Chapel Hill: Univ. of North Carolina Press, 1939. 142p.

Richardson, Marilyn (b. 1942), historical essayist. Graduate, Bancroft Country Day School, Worcester, Mass., 1960; book designer, Boston; Lecturer in Humanities, Boston Univ., 1966–70; educational consultant, 1970–73; Instructor in Humanities, Univ. of Massachusetts, Boston, 1973–80; Asst. Prof. of Exposition and Rhetoric, Writing Program, Dept. of Humanities, Massachusetts Institute of Technology, 1980––.

Black Women and Religion: A Bibliography. Illus. Boston: G. K. Hall, 1980. 139p.

Robeson, Eslanda (1896–1965), essayist, biographer. Attended Kennedy School of Missions, Hartford, Conn., Seminary Foundation, 1943–44; candidate, Ph.D. degree.

African Journey. Illus. Bibliog. New York: John Day Co., 1945. 154p.

Paul Robeson, Negro. Illus. New York and London: Harper and Brothers, 1930. 178p.

Robinson, William Henry (b. 1922), critic, biographer, editor. Born in Newport, R.I.; M.A., Boston Univ., 1957; Ph.D., Harvard Univ., 1964; taught
at Boston Univ., 1966–68; Prof. of English and American Literature,
1970––, and Director of Black Studies, 1970–81, Rhode Island College.

Black New England Letters: The Uses of Writings in Black New England.
Illus. Bibliog. Boston: Boston Public Library, 1977. 146p.

Ed., *Critical Essays on Phillis Wheatley.* Bibliog. Boston: G. K. Hall,
1982. 236p.

*Early Black American Poets: Selections with Biographical and Critical
Introductions.* Bibliog. Dubuque, Iowa: W. C. Brown Co., 1969. 275p.

Phillis Wheatley: A Bio-Bibliography. Boston: G. K. Hall, 1981. 166p.

Phillis Wheatley and Her Writings. Illus. Bibliog. New York: Garland
Publishing, 1984. 464p.

Phillis Wheatley in the Black American Beginnings. Bibliog. Detroit:
Broadside Press, 1975. 95p.

Rollin, Frances Anne (Rollin, Frank A. [pseud.]), biographer. Born free in
South Carolina; lived in Boston, fall, 1867–July, 1868, while writing
biography of Martin R. Delany; boarded with a family on Blossom St.,
near black community.

Life and Public Services of Martin R. Delany. 1883 ed.; rpt. New York:
Arno Press, 1969. 367p.

Rollins, Bryant (b. 1937), novelist, poet, biographer. Grew up in Roxbury
section of Boston; B.A., Northeastern Univ., 1960; was reporter, *Boston
Globe*, and editor, *Bay State Banner.*

Danger Song. Intro. by James A. Miller. 1967 ed.; rpt. New York:
Collier Books, 1971. 316p.

*Greens and Blues and All the Rhythms In Between: Poetry for My
Friends.* Harlem, N.Y.: Privately printed, 1973. 22p.

Of Minnie the Moocher & Me. With Cab Calloway. Illus. New York:
Crowell, 1976. 282p.

Roper, Moses (b. 1816?), author of slave narrative. Born a slave in North
Carolina; escaped by ship from Savannah, Georgia, 1834; stayed in
N.H., Sudbury and Ludlow, Vt., Brookline, Mass., and Boston,
1834–35; attended "coloured church" on Belknap St. (now Joy St.),
Boston; left when slavehunter inquired of him at shop of employment;
went to England.

*A Narrative of the Adventures and Escape of Moses Roper, from
American Slavery; With a Preface by the Rev. T. Price, D.D.* Illus. 2nd
ed., 1838; rpt. New York: Negro Universities Press, 1970. 108p.

Rushing, Byron (b. 1942), essayist. Attended Harvard Univ., 1960–63; community organizer, Boston, 1964–72; President, Museum of Afro-American History, 1972––; State Representative, 1983––.

Archeological Reconnaissance Survey of the Southwest Corridor Project Area (Part One). With Beth Bower. Illus. Boston: Massachusetts Bay Transportation Authority, Southwest Corridor Project, 1979. 97p.

Black Heritage Trail. Illus. U.S. Department of the Interior, National Park Service, Boston African American National Historic Site, 15 State St., Boston, MA 02109. 1st ed., 1981; 2nd ed., 1983. 10p.

The Hill: The Middle Classes Come to Roxbury: 1870––. Exhibition catalog. Illus. Boston: Museum of Afro-American History, 1975. 19p.

The Lost and Found Paintings of Allan Rohan Crite. Exhibition catalog with comments by Allan Rohan Crite. Boston: Museum of Afro-American History, 1982. 8p.

Roxbury Yesteryears. Exhibition catalog. Illus. Boston: Museum of Afro-American History and Museum of National Center of Afro-American Artists, 1974. 33p.

Russell, Bill (b. 1934), memoirist. Professional basketball player with Boston Celtics, 1956–69.

Go Up for Glory. As told to William McSweeny. New York: Coward-McCann, 1966. 224p.

Second Wind: The Memoirs of an Opinionated Man. With Taylor French. New York: Random House, 1979. 265p.

Sanchez, Sonia (b. 1934), poet, short story writer, playwright, editor. Assoc. Prof. of Literature and Creative Writing, Amherst College, 1973–75.

The Adventures of Fathead, Smallhead, and Squarehead. Illus. by Taiwo DuVall. New York: Third Press, 1973. 29p.

A Blues Book for Blue Black Magical Women. Poems. Detroit: Broadside Press, 1974. 62p.

Home Coming: Poems. Intro. by Don L. Lee. Detroit: Broadside Press, 1969. 32p.

It's a New Day: Poems for Young Brothas and Sistuhs. Detroit: Broadside Press, 1971. 29p.

I've Been a Woman: New and Selected Poems. Sausalito, Calif.: Black Scholar Press, 1978. 101p.

Love Poems. Illus. New York: Third Press, 1973. 101p.

A Sound Investment: Short Stories for Young Readers. Illus. by Larry Crowe. Chicago: Third World Press, 1980. 25p.

We a BaddDDD People. Poems. Intro. by Dudley Randall. Detroit: Broadside Press, 1970. 72p.

Ed., *We Be Word Sorcerers: 25 Stories by Black Americans.* New York: Bantam Books, 1973. 284p.

Schuyler, George S. (1895–1977), novelist, autobiographer, journalist. Born in Providence, R.I.

Black and Conservative: The Autobiography of George S. Schuyler. New Rochelle, N.Y.: Arlington House, 1966. 362p.

Black No More: Being an Account of the Strange and Wonderful Workings of Science in the Land of the Free, A.D. 1933–1940. A novel. Intro. by Charles R. Larson. c1931; rpt. New York: Collier Books, 1971. 222p.

Slaves Today: A Story of Liberia. A novel. 1931 ed.; rpt. College Park, Md.: McGrath Publishing Co., 1969. 290p.

About George S. Schuyler

Peplow, Michael W. *George S. Schuyler.* Bibliog. Boston: Twayne Publishers, 1980. 144p.

Seale, Bobby (b. 1936), social activist historian, autobiographer. In prison and on trial on murder-kidnapping charges in New Haven, Conn., 1971; charges dismissed after hung jury.

A Lonely Rage: The Autobiography of Bobby Seale. Foreword by James Baldwin. New York: Times Books, 1978. 238p.

Seize the Time: The Story of the Black Panther Party and Huey P. Newton. New York: Random House, 1970. 429p.

About Bobby Seale

Marine, Gene. *The Black Panthers.* New York: New American Library, 1969. 224p.

Sellers, Cleveland (b. 1944), social activist memoirist. Studied for Master's degree in education at Harvard Graduate School of Education, 1969–70.

The River of No Return: The Autobiography of a Black Militant and the Life and Death of SNCC. With Robert Terrell. New York: Morrow, 1973. 279p.

Simmons, Judy Dothard (b. 1944), poet. Born in Westerly, R.I.

Judith's Blues. Detroit: Broadside Press, 1973. 22p.

Smith, Barbara (b. 1946), editor, essayist. B.A., Mt. Holyoke College, 1969; doctoral student, Univ. of Connecticut; taught English at Emerson College, Boston.

Ed., *All the Women Are White, All the Blacks Are Men, But Some of Us Are Brave: Black Women's Studies.* With Gloria T. Hull and Patricia Bell Scott. Illus. Bibliog. Old Westbury, N.Y.: Feminist Press, 1982. 401p.

Ed., *Home Girls: A Black Feminist Anthology.* New York: Kitchen Table, Women of Color Press, 1983. 377p.

Smith, Daniel (b. 1935), novelist. Born in Boston; has lived in Billerica, Boston, Mansfield, and Dracut, Mass.; B.S., 1966, M.Ed., 1967, Boston Univ.; Vice-Principal, Dracut High School, 1972--.

A Walk in the City. c1971; rpt. New York: Manor Books, 1974. 337p.

Smith, Gary (b. 1949), essayist, editor, poet. B.A., Boston Univ., 1973.

Songs for My Fathers. Illus. Detroit: Lotus Press, 1984. 78p.

Smith, James Lindsay (d. 1883?), autobiographer. Escaped from slavery in Virginia to Springfield, Mass., 1838; educated in Wilbraham, Mass.; travelled a year in Mass. and Conn. speaking at antislavery meetings; settled in Norwich, Conn.; boot and shoe maker and Methodist minister.

Autobiography of James L. Smith, Including, Also, Reminiscences of Slave Life, Recollections of the War, Education of Freedmen, Causes of the Exodus, etc. Illus. 1881 ed.; rpt. New York: Negro Universities Press, 1969. 150p. Rpt. in *Five Black Lives: The Autobiographies of Venture Smith, James Mars, William Grimes, The Rev. G. W. Offley, James L. Smith,* Intro. by Arna Bontemps (Middletown, Conn.: Wesleyan Univ. Press, 1971), p. 139–240.

Smith, Venture (1729?-1805), author of slave narrative. Born in Guinea, son of tribal chief; at eight brought with master, ship's steward, on slave ship to Rhode Island; slave servant at Fishers Island, Stonington Point, and Hartford, Conn.; bought freedom for self and family; settled on farm in Haddam Neck, owned fishing and coastal cargo vessels; buried in cemetery of First Congregational Church, East Haddam.

A Narrative of the Life and Adventures of Venture, A Native of Africa: But Resident Above Sixty Years in the United States of America. 1798 ed.; rpt. in Dorothy Porter, *Early Negro Writing 1760-1837* (Boston: Beacon Press, 1971), p. 538–558; 1798 ed., "Revised and Republished with Traditions by H. M. Selden," 1897; rpt. in *Five Black Lives: The Autobiographies of Venture Smith, James Mars, William Grimes, The Rev. G. W. Offley, James L. Smith,* Intro. by Arna Bontemps (Middletown, Conn.: Wesleyan Univ. Press, 1971), p. 1–25; "Traditions," p. 26–34.

Smitherman, Geneva (b. 1940), essayist. Lecturer in Afro-American Studies, Harvard Univ., 1971–73.

Black Language and Culture: Sounds of Soul. Bibliog. New York: Harper and Row, 1975. 33p.

Snowden, Frank M., Jr. (b. 1911), cultural historian. B.A., 1932, M.A., 1933, Ph.D., 1944, Harvard Univ.

Before Color Prejudice: The Ancient View of Blacks. Illus. Bibliog. Cambridge, Mass.: Harvard Univ. Press, 1983. 164p.

Southern, Eileen Jackson (b. 1920), music historian. M.A., Harvard Univ., 1976; Prof. of Music and Afro-American Studies, Harvard Univ., 1976––.

Biographical Dictionary of Afro-American and African Musicians. Bibliog. Westport, Conn.: Greenwood Press, 1982. 478p.

The Music of Black Americans: A History. Illus. Bibliog. and discography. New York: Norton, 1971. 552p.

Stamper, Corrine (b. 1947), poet. B.S., Northeastern Univ., 1973. Has taught in Boston public schools.

The Resistance. By Sam Stamper [pseud.]. Photos by Joe Tasby. New York: Sesame Press, 1973. 41p.

Sam, Stone, Cold, Silk: Poems. By Sam Stamper [pseud.]. Illus. Boston: Art Ad Corp., 1972. 94p.

Stevens, Walter J. (b. 1877), autobiographer. Born in Boston of black father and white mother, grew up in West End, attended Charles Street A.M.E. Church; Steward at Signet Club, Harvard Univ.; tutored by Profs. Hugo Munsterberg and G. L. Kittredge; personal secretary to Edward A. Filene, president of department store; left Boston in World War One.

Chip on My Shoulder: Autobiography of Walter J. Stevens. Illus. Boston: Meador Publishing Co., 1946. 315p.

Stewart, Maria W. (1803–1879), lecturer. Born in Hartford, Conn.; orphan at five, bound out as servant in clergyman's family until fifteen, attended Sabbath Schools until twenty, married in 1826, widowed in 1829; her lecture in Boston in 1832 the first public lecture by an American woman on a political theme.

An Address Delivered at the African Masonic Hall, Boston, February 27, 1833. Rpt. in Dorothy Porter, *Early Negro Writing 1760–1837* (Boston: Beacon Press, 1971), p. 129–135; rpt. from *Productions of Maria W. Stewart* (Boston: Friends of Freedom and Virtue, 1835), p. 63–72.

A Lecture by Maria W. Stewart, given at Franklin Hall, Boston, September 21, 1832. Rpt. in Dorothy Porter, *Early Negro Writing 1760–1837* (Boston: Beacon Press, 1971), p. 136–140; rpt. from *The Liberator*, Vol. 2,. No. 46 (Nov. 17, 1832), p. 183.

Religion and the Pure Principles of Morality, the Sure Foundation on Which We Must Build. Pamphlet, Boston, October, 1831; rpt. in Dorothy Porter, *Early Negro Writing 1760–1837* (Boston: Beacon Press, 1971), p. 460–471.

Stone, Chuck (b. 1924), novelist, essayist. Youth in Hartford, Conn.; B.A., Wesleyan Univ., Conn., 1948.

King Strut. Indianapolis, Ind.: Bobbs-Merrill, 1970. 357p.

Stroyer, Jacob (b. 1849), author of slave narrative. Born a slave in South Carolina; freed in 1865 upon news of Emancipation Proclamation; went to Worcester, Mass., 1869, where studied in evening schools and academy and became minister, African Methodist Episcopal church; settled as pastor in Salem.

My Life in the South. 4th ed., enlarged, 1898; rpt. in William Loren Katz, ed., *Five Slave Narratives: A Compendium* (New York: Arno Press, 1968), 100p.

Taylor, Clyde R. (b. 1931), editor, critic. Born in Boston; Assoc. Prof. of English, Tufts Univ., 1982––.

Ed., *Vietnam and Black America: An Anthology of Protest and Resistance.* Bibliog. Garden City, N.Y.: Anchor Press, 1973. 335p.

Taylor, Susie King (1848–19––?), memoirist. Born a slave in Georgia; laundress, cook, and nurse with colored regiment, Union army, 1862–65; domestic in white family, Rye Beach, N.H., 1873; settled in Boston, 1874; domestic, 1874–79; helped organize in 1886 and was officer in Corps 67, Women's Relief Corps, G.A.R., in existence until at least 1902.

Reminiscences of My Life in Camp: With the 33d United States Colored Troops Late 1st S.C. Volunteers. Intro. by Thomas Wentworth Higginson. Illus. Boston: Published by the Author, 1902. 82p. Xerox facsimile.

Terrell, Mary Church (1863–1954), essayist, autobiographer. Born free in Tennessee; lectured in Boston, probably often, from about 1930–60.

A Colored Woman in a White World. Illus. Washington, D.C.: Ransdell, Inc., 1940. 436p.

Susie King Taylor

(Reproduced from *Reminiscences of My Life in Camp*, 1902)

Sterling, Dorothy. *Black Foremothers: Three Lives.* Intro. by Margaret Walker. Illus. by Judith Eloise Hooper. Bibliog. Old Westbury, N.Y.: Feminist Press, 1979. 167p.

------------. *Lift Every Voice: The Lives of Booker T. Washington, W. E. B. Du Bois, Mary Church Terrell, and James Weldon Johnson.* With Benjamin Quarles. Illus. by Ernest Crichlow. Garden City, N.Y.: Doubleday, 1965. 116p.

Thelwell, Michael (b. 1938), novelist, essayist. Prof. of Afro-American Studies, Univ. of Massachusetts, Amherst.

The Harder They Come. A novel. New York: Grove Press (distributed by Random House), 1980. 399p.

Thomas, Ted, Jr. (b. 1947), poet. Grew up in Boston; Diploma, Dorchester High School; B.A., 1974, M.A., 1985, Northeastern Univ.; Director of Youth Services, City Mission Society; Consultant in Language Arts, Boston Public Schools.

Annie With The Wig On. Illus. Boston: Unity Press, 1976. 48p. Distributed by the Author, 37 Jamaica St., Jamaica Plain, MA 02130.

The Little Blue Book of Love. With Sara Ting. Cordillera Press, 4 Marshall Rd., Natick, MA 01760. 1985. 65p.

Thompson, John (b. 1812), author of slave narrative. Escaped slave from Maryland; sailed as steward on whaling ship *Milwood* from New Bedford, Mass., on two-year voyage to Africa and Indian Ocean; was in Worcester, 1856.

The Life of John Thompson, A Fugitive Slave; Containing His History of 25 Years in Bondage, and His Providential Escape. Written by Himself. 1856 ed.; rpt. New York: Negro Universities Press, 1968. 143p.

Thurman, Howard (1899-1981), essayist, autobiographer. Dean, Marsh Chapel, 1953–64; Prof. of Spiritual Disciplines and Resources, 1953–65; University Minister-at-Large, 1964–65, Boston Univ.

The Creative Encounter: An Interpretation of Religion and the Social Witness. 1954 ed.; rpt. Richmond, Ind.: Friends United Press, 1972. 153p.

Deep Is the Hunger: Meditations for Apostles of Sensitiveness. 1951 ed.; rpt. Richmond, Ind.: Friends United Press, 1973. 212p.

Deep River: Reflections on the Religious Insight of Certain of the Negro Spirituals. Illus. by Elizabeth Orton Jones. c1944, 1955; rpt. Port Washington, N.Y.: Kennikat Press, 1969. 93p.

Disciplines of the Spirit. New York: Harper and Row, 1963. 127p.

The Growing Edge. 1956 ed.; rpt. Richmond, Ind.: Friends United Press, 1974. 181p.

The Inward Journey. 1961 ed.; rpt. Richmond, Ind.: Friends United Press, 1971. 155p.

Jesus and the Disinherited. New York: Abingdon-Cokesbury Press, 1949. 112p.

Meditations of the Heart. New York: Harper, 1953. 216p.

The Search for Common Ground: An Inquiry Into the Basis of Man's Experience of Community. Bibliog. New York: Harper and Row, 1971. 108p.

Ed., *A Track to the Water's Edge: The Olive Schreiner Reader.* Illus. Bibliog. New York: Harper and Row, 1973. 198p.

With Head and Heart: The Autobiography of Howard Thurman. Illus. New York: Harcourt Brace Jovanovich, 1979. 274p.

About Howard Thurman

Smith, Luther E. *Howard Thurman: The Mystic as Prophet.* Illus. Bibliog. Washington, D.C.: University Press of America, 1981. 191p.

Toomer, Jean (1894–1967), novelist, short story writer, poet, playwright, essayist. Attended Massachusetts College of Agriculture, Amherst, briefly in fall, 1915; lived in fraternity house; temporary captain of college football team.

Cane. Foreword by Waldo Frank. c1923; rpt. New York: University Place Press, 1967. 239p.

The Wayward and the Seeking: A Collection of Writings by Jean Toomer. Ed. and intro. by Darwin T. Turner. Washington, D.C.: Howard Univ. Press, 1980. 450p.

About Jean Toomer

Benson, Brian Joseph and **Mabel Mayle Dillard.** *Jean Toomer.* Bibliog. Boston: Twayne Publishers, 1980. 152p.

Durham, Frank, ed. *The Merrill Studies in Cane.* Bibliog. Columbus, Ohio: Merrill Publishing Co., 1971. 113p.

Gysin, Fritz. *The Grotesque in American Negro Fiction: Jean Toomer, Richard Wright, and Ralph Ellison.* Bibliog. Bern, Switzerland: Francke, 1975. 330p.

McKay, Nellie Y. *Jean Toomer, Artist: A Study of His Literary Life and Work, 1894–1936.* Illus. Bibliog. Chapel Hill: Univ. of North Carolina Press, 1984. 262p.

Rusch, Frederick Lunning. *Every Atom Belonging to Me as Good Belongs to You: Jean Toomer and His Bringing Together of the Scattered Parts.* Bibliog. Thesis—State Univ. of New York at Albany, College of Arts and Sciences, Dept. of English, 1976. 383p. Ann Arbor, Mich.: University Microfilms, 1978. Microfilm, 1 reel, 35mm.

Turner, Darwin T. *In a Minor Chord: Three Afro-American Writers and Their Search for Identity.* Pref. by Harry T. Moore. Bibliog. Carbondale: Southern Illinois Univ. Press, 1971. 153p.

Trotter, James M. (1842–1892), music historian. Second Lieutenant, 55th Massachusetts Regiment, a black unit, in Civil War; settled in Boston in 1865 when mustered out there and rewarded for war service with appointment to post office; resigned in 1882 as protest when white man promoted over him.

Music and Some Highly Musical People. Containing Brief Chapters on I. A Description of Music. II. The Music of Nature. III. A Glance at the History of Music. IV. The Power, Beauty, and Uses of Music; Following Which Are Given Sketches of the Lives of Remarkable Musicians of the Colored Race. With Portraits, and an Appendix Containing Copies of Music Composed by Colored Men. 1881 ed.; rpt. New York and London: Johnson Reprint Corp., 1968. 353p.; Appendix, 152p.

Trotter, William Monroe (1872–1934), journalist. Son of James M. Trotter, grew up in Hyde Park section of Boston; B.A., 1895, M.A., 1896, Harvard Univ.; founded and edited *The Guardian* in Boston, 1901–34.

About William Monroe Trotter

Fox, Stephen R. *The Guardian of Boston: William Monroe Trotter.* Illus. Bibliog. New York: Atheneum, 1970. 307p.

Walcott, Derek (b. 1930), poet, playwright, essayist. Teaches poetry and playwriting, Boston Univ.

Another Life. New York: Farrar, Straus and Giroux, 1973. 151p.

Dream on Monkey Mountain, and Other Plays. New York: Farrar, Straus and Giroux, 1970. 326p.

The Fortunate Traveller. New York: Farrar, Straus and Giroux, 1981. 99p.

Midsummer. New York: Farrar, Straus and Giroux, 1984. 78p.

Sea Grapes. New York: Farrar, Straus and Giroux, 1976. 83p.

Selected Poems. New York: Farrar, Straus, 1964. 85p.

The Star-Apple Kingdom. New York: Farrar, Straus and Giroux, 1979. 57p.

About Derek Walcott

Goldstraw, Irma E. *Derek Walcott: An Annotated Bibliography of His Works, 1944–1980.* New York: Garland Publishing, 1984. 238p.

Hamner, Robert D. *Derek Walcott.* Illus. Bibliog. Boston: Twayne Publishers, 1981. 175p.

Walker, Alice (b. 1944), novelist, short story writer, poet, essayist. Fellow, Radcliffe Institute, 1971–73; taught at Univ. of Massachusetts, Boston, and Wellesley College, 1972.

Good Night, Willie Lee, I'll See You in the Morning: Poems. New York: Dial Press, 1979. 53p.

Ed., *I Love Myself When I Am Laughing. . .And Then Again When I Am Looking Mean and Impressive: A Zora Neale Hurston Reader.* Intro. by Mary Helen Washington. Illus. Bibliog. Old Westbury, N.Y.: Feminist Press, 1979. 313p.

In Love and Trouble: Stories of Black Women. New York: Harcourt Brace Jovanovich, 1973. 138p.

In Search of Our Mothers' Gardens: Womanist Prose. Bibliog. San Diego and New York: Harcourt Brace Jovanovich, 1983. 397p.

Langston Hughes, American Poet. Illus. by Don Miller. New York: Crowell, 1974. 33p.

Meridian. New York: Harcourt Brace Jovanovich, 1976. 228p.

Once: Poems. New York: Harcourt, Brace and World, 1968. 81p.

Revolutionary Petunias and Other Poems. New York: Harcourt Brace Jovanovich, 1973. 70p.

The Color Purple. New York: Harcourt Brace Jovanovich, 1982. 245p.

The Third Life of Grange Copeland. New York: Harcourt Brace Jovanovich, 1970. 247p.

You Can't Keep a Good Woman Down: Stories. New York: Harcourt Brace Jovanovich, 1981. 167p.

Walker, David (1785–1830), militant abolitionist essayist and speaker. Born in North Carolina of free mother and slave father, took mother's status in accordance with law; settled in Boston; in 1827 became dealer in old clothes on Brattle Street; after publication of his *Appeal* in 1829, reward offered in Georgia of $1000 for Walker dead and $10,000 alive; died mysteriously in 1830, possibly poisoned.

David Walker's Appeal, in Four Articles, Together with a Preamble, to the Coloured Citizens of the World, but in Particular, and Very Expressly, to Those of the United States of America. Ed. and intro. by Charles M. Wiltse. Bibliog. 1829 ed.; rpt. New York: Hill and Wang, 1965. 78p.

About David Walker

Aptheker, Herbert. *One Continual Cry: David Walker's Appeal to the Colored Citizens of the World, 1829–1830; Its Setting and Its Meaning, Together with the Full Text of the Third, and Last, Edition of the Appeal.* Bibliog. New York: Published for A.I.M.S. by Humanities Press, 1965. 150p.

Washington, Mary Helen (b. 1941), editor, critic. Assoc. Prof. of English, Univ. of Massachusetts, Boston.

Ed., *Black-Eyed Susans: Classic Stories By and About Black Women.* Bibliog. Garden City, N.Y.: Anchor Books, 1975. 163p.

Ed., *Midnight Birds: Stories By Contemporary Black Women Writers.* Garden City, N.Y.: Anchor Books, 1980. 274p.

Wells, Ida B. (1862–1931), journalist, autobiographer. Born a slave in Mississippi; lectured against lynching, Tremont Temple and Ladies' Physiological Institute, Boston, and throughout New England, 1892–93.

About Ida B. Wells

Sterling, Dorothy. *Black Foremothers: Three Lives.* Intro. by Margaret Walker. Illus. by Judith Eloise Hooper. Bibliog. Old Westbury, N.Y.: Feminist Press, 1979. 167p.

Wesley, Charles H. (b. 1891), historian, biographer. M.A., Yale Univ., 1913; Ph.D., Harvard Univ., 1925.

History of the Improved Benevolent and Protective Order of Elks of the World, 1898–1954. Illus. Washington, D.C.: Association for the Study of Negro Life and History, 1955. 506p.

In Freedom's Footsteps: From the African Background to the Civil War. Illus. Bibliog. International Library of Afro-American Life and History, Vol. 6. Rev. ed.; Cornwells Heights, Pa.: Publishers Agency, 1976. 307p.

Prince Hall: Life and Legacy. Illus. Bibliog. 2nd ed.; United Supreme Council, Southern Jurisdiction, Prince Hall Affiliation, P.O. Box 2959, Washington, D.C. 20013. 1983. 237p.

The Quest for Equality: From Civil War to Civil Rights. Illus. Bibliog. International Library of Afro-American Life and History, Vol. 9. Rev. ed.; Cornwells Heights, Pa.: Publishers Agency, 1976. 307p.

West, Dorothy (b. 1910), novelist, short story writer, editor, columnist. Born and raised in Boston, educated at Girls Latin School and Boston Univ.; lives in Oak Bluffs, Martha's Vineyard, writes weekly column in *Vineyard Gazette.*

Interview with Dorothy West: May 6, 1978. Conducted by Genii Guinier. Illus. Cambridge, Mass.: Schlesinger Library, Radcliffe College, 1981. 75p.

The Living Is Easy. Afterword by Adelaide M. Cromwell. 1948 ed.; rpt. Old Westbury, N.Y.: Feminist Press, 1982. 364p.

The Living Is Easy. Intro. by William H. Robinson. 1948 ed.; rpt. New York: Arno Press, 1969. 347p.

Wheatley, Phillis (1753?–1784), poet. Taken to Boston on ship from Africa, probably in "parcel of likely Negroes" in 1761; slave servant in household of John Wheatley, Boston merchant; baptized in Old South Meeting House, 1771; manumitted by October, 1773; married John Peters, free black, 1778; had three children; at death reduced to poverty as domestic in black boarding house in run-down section of Boston.

Life and Works of Phillis Wheatley; Containing Her Complete Poetical Works, Numerous Letters, and a Complete Biography of This Famous Poet of a Century and a Half Ago. By G. Herbert Renfro. Also, *A Sketch of the Life of Mr. Renfro*, by Leila Amos Pendleton. Illus. 1916 ed.; rpt. Miami, Fla.: Mnemosyne Publishing Co., 1969. 112p.

Memoir and Poems of Phillis Wheatley, a Native African and a Slave. Also, *Poems by a Slave*, by George M. Horton, p. 117–155. 3rd ed., 1838; rpt. Miami, Fla.: Mnemosyne Publishing Co., 1969. 155p.

Phillis Wheatley (Phillis Peters): Poems and Letters. Ed. by Charles Frederick Heartman. With an appreciation by Arthur A. Schomburg. 1st collected ed., 1915; rpt. Miami, Fla.: Mnemosyne Publishing Co., 1969. 111p.

The Poems of Phillis Wheatley. Illus. Ed. and intro. by Julian D. Mason, Jr. Chapel Hill: Univ. of North Carolina Press, 1966. 113p.

Poems on Various Subjects, Religious and Moral, by Phillis Wheatley. 1786 ed.; rpt. New York: AMS Press, 1976. 66p.

About Phillis Wheatley

Allen, William G. *Wheatley, Banneker, and Horton; With Selections from the Poetical Works of Wheatley and Horton.* 1849 ed.; rpt. Freeport, N.Y.: Books for Libraries Press, 1970. 48p.

Fuller, Miriam Morris. *Phillis Wheatley, America's First Black Poetess.* Illus. by Victor Mays. Champaign, Ill.: Garrard Publishing Co., 1971. 94p.

Graham, Shirley. *The Story of Phillis Wheatley.* Illus. by Robert Burns. New York: J. Messner, 1949. 176p.

Richmond, Merle A. *Bid the Vassal Soar: Interpretive Essays on the Life and Poetry of Phillis Wheatley (ca. 1753–1784) and George Moses Horton (ca. 1797–1883).* Washington, D.C.: Howard Univ. Press, 1974. 216p.

Robinson, William Henry, ed. *Critical Essays on Phillis Wheatley.* Bibliog. Boston: G. K. Hall, 1982. 236p.

Robinson, William Henry. *Phillis Wheatley: A Bio-Bibliography.* Boston: G. K. Hall, 1981. 166p.

----------. *Phillis Wheatley and Her Writings.* Illus. Bibliog. New York: Garland Publishing, 1984. 464p.

----------. *Phillis Wheatley in the Black American Beginnings.* Bibliog. Detroit: Broadside Press, 1975. 95p.

Williams, George Washington (1849–1891), historian. Member, First Baptist Church, Watertown, Mass., in period 1870–74; graduate, Newton, Mass., Theological Institution, 1874; pastor, Twelfth Baptist Church, Boston, 1874–75; attorney, Boston, 1883–84; spent summers in Plymouth, Mass.; lived in Worcester, 1888–90.

1862—Emancipation Day—1884. The Negro as a Political Problem. Oration, by the Hon. George W. Williams at the Asbury Church, Washington, D.C., April 16, 1884. 1884 ed.; Chicago: Library Resources, Inc., 1972. 40p. Microbook Library of American Civilization, LAC 40078, Microfilm.

History of the Negro Race in America from 1619 to 1880. Negroes as Slaves, as Soldiers, and as Citizens; Together with a Preliminary Consideration of the Unity of the Human Family, an Historical Sketch of Africa, and an Account of the Negro Governments of Sierra Leone and Liberia. 2 vols. in 1; Vol. 1 (1619–1800), 481p.; Vol. 2 (1800–1880), 611p. Illus. 1883 ed.; rpt. New York: Arno Press, 1968.

A History of the Negro Troops in the War of the Rebellion, 1861–1865, Preceded by a Review of the Military Services of Negroes in Ancient and Modern Times. Illus. 1888 ed.; Chicago: Library Resources, Inc., 1972. 353p. Microbook Library of American Civilization, LAC 12901, Microfilm.

About George Washington Williams

Franklin, John Hope. *George Washington Williams: The Massachusetts Years.* Rpt. from *Proceedings of American Antiquarian Society,* Vol. 92, Part 2 (October 1982), p. 243–263. Worcester, Mass.: American Antiquarian Society, 1983.

Willie, Charles V. (b. 1927), essayist, editor. Prof. of Education and Urban Studies, Harvard Univ., 1974--.

Ed., *The Family Life of Black People.* Bibliog. Columbus, Ohio: Merrill Publishing Co., 1970. 341p.

Wilson, Harriet E. (b. 1827 or 1828?), novelist. Probably born in N.H., perhaps Milford; servant in family, impairing her health; lived with white family in Milford, 1850; worked as straw hat maker in central Mass.; married in Milford, 1851; destitute and alone, placed son, born in 1852, in white foster family; probably lived in Boston when published her novel there in 1859; son died in 1860.

Our Nig; or, Sketches from the Life of a Free Black, In a Two-Story White House, North. Showing that Slavery's Shadows Fall Even There, by "Our Nig." Ed. and intro. by Henry Louis Gates, Jr. Bibliog. New York: Vintage Books, 1983. 140p.

Woodson, Carter G. (1875–1950), historian. Ph.D., Harvard Univ., 1912.

The African Background Outlined: or, Handbook for the Study of the Negro. Maps. Bibliog. c1936; rpt. New York: New American Library, 1969. 478p.

A Century of Negro Migration. Maps. Washington, D.C.: Association for the Study of Negro Life and History, 1918. 221p.

The Education of the Negro Prior to 1861. Bibliog. 2nd ed., 1919; rpt. New York: Arno Press, 1968. 454p.

The History of the Negro Church. Illus. Washington, D.C.: Associated Publishers, 1921. 330p. Xerox facsimile.

The Mind of the Negro as Reflected in Letters Written During the Crisis, 1800–1860. Bibliog. 1926 ed.; rpt. New York: Negro Universities Press, 1969. 672p.

The Mis-Education of the Negro. 1933 ed.; rpt. New York: AMS Press, 1972. 207p.

Wright, Nathan, Jr. (b. 1923), essayist. B.D., Episcopal Theological School, Cambridge, Mass., 1950; S.T.M., Harvard Univ., 1951; Ed.M., State Teachers College, Boston, 1962; Ed.D., Harvard Univ., 1964; was Rector, St. Cyprian's Episcopal Church, Protestant Chaplain, Long Island Hospital, Boston.

Let's Work Together. New York: Hawthorn Books, 1968. 271p.

Ready to Riot. Illus. Bibliog. New York: Holt, Rinehart and Winston, 1968. 148p.

II

AFRO-AMERICAN WRITERS ASSOCIATED WITH NEW ENGLAND NOT REPRESENTED WITH BOOKS BY OR ABOUT THEM IN THE
Collection of Afro-American Literature

Addison, Lloyd (b. 1931), editor, poet. Born in Boston.

Alexson, Sam (b. 1852), autobiographer. Ex-slave from South Carolina, Confederate officer in Civil War; moved in 1876 to "Spring Lake, New England," probably Windsor, Vt., where worked as laborer.

Anderson, Marian (b. 1902), autobiographer. Lives in Danbury, Conn.

Bass, George (b. 1938), playwright, poet. John Golden Fellow, School of Drama, Yale Univ., 1966–68; Assoc. Prof. of Theater Arts and Afro-American Studies, Brown Univ.

Blue, Cecil (b. 1903), short story writer. M.A., Harvard Univ., 1926.

Bonner, Marita (1899–1971), playwright, short story writer, poet. Born in Dorchester section of Boston; attended Brookline, Mass., High School; B.A., Radcliffe College, 1922.

Bowen, Robert T. (b. 1936), poet, critic. Born in New Haven, Conn.; Diploma, Hillhouse High School, New Haven, 1954; B.A., Univ. of Connecticut, 1958.

Braddan, William S. (b. 1872), autobiographer, memoirist. Pastor, Salem Baptist Church, New Bedford, Mass., 1892; studied for ministry at Newton Theological Institution, 1893–95.

Brown, Azariah, autobiographer. Camp meeting minister in Connecticut and Massachusetts, late 19th century.

Brown, Charlotte Hawkins (1883–1961), novelist, essayist. Attended Cambridge, Mass., elementary school, Boston-Allston Grammar School, Cambridge English High School; B.A., State Normal School, Salem, 1901.

Brown, Rose Butler (b. 1897), autobiographer. Youth in Boston and
Newport, R.I.; educated at Rhode Island Normal School, Univ. of
Rhode Island, and Harvard Univ.

Bullock, Samuel Howard, memoirist. Minister of Baptist church in Roxbury
section of Boston, 1939–48.

Bunche, Ralph (1914–1971), essayist. M.A., 1928, Ph.D., 1934, Harvard Univ.

Burton, Annie L. (b. 1858), memoirist. After slavery in Alabama, had jobs
and business ventures in Newport, R.I., and Boston.

Chester, Henry L. (b. 1896), memoirist. Worked in Newport, R.I.

Coppin, Fanny M. Jackson (1836–1913), memoirist. A slave in Washington,
D.C., purchased by New England family; lived in New Bedford, Mass.,
and Newport, R.I.

Cox, Joseph Mason Andrew (b. 1923), poet, novelist, playwright. Born
in Boston.

Christian, Malcolm Henry (b. 1904), autobiographer. Worked in Massachusetts before settling in Chicago in 1927.

Cromwell, Adelaide M. (Gulliver) (b. 1919), social historian. B.A., Smith
College, 1940; Ph.D., Radcliffe College, 1952; Instructor in Sociology,
Smith College, 1944–46; Prof. of Sociology and Director of Afro-
American Studies, Boston Univ.

Cuney, Waring (b. 1906), poet. Attended New England Conservatory
of Music

DeCoy, Robert H. (b. 1920), playwright, radio documentary writer, essayist.
M.F.A., Yale Univ., 1951.

Dixon, George (b. 1870), essayist, memoirist. Spent early years in Boston.

Drafts, Gene (b. 1946), poet, journalist. Born in Boston, attended Massachusetts Bay Community College, Boston.

Fields, Alonzo (b. 1900), memoirist. Studied at New England Conservatory
of Music; was butler for president of Massachusetts Institute of
Technology.

Foote, Julia A. J. (b. 1823), autobiographer. Called into religious life
after mystical experience in Boston; became African Methodist Episcopal
evangelist.

Geary, Bruce (b. 1944), poet, playwright. Born in Roxbury section of Boston; has been serving life sentence, Norfolk, Mass., state prison.

Goncalves, Joe (b. 1937), poet, editor of black poetry journal. Born in Boston.

Grimké, Archibald H. (1849–1930), journalist, biographer. LL.B., Harvard Law School, 1874; attorney in Boston; editor, *The Hub*, weekly newspaper, 1883–85; freelance writer, *Boston Traveler, Boston Herald, Atlantic Monthly*.

Harris, Charles Jacob (b. 1885), memoirist. Piano accompanist to Roland Hayes, concert singer, in Boston and on tours in New England, 1911–17.

Harrison, Samuel (1818–1900), autobiographer. Minister in Pittsfield and Springfield, Mass.; Hartford, Conn.; Newport, R.I.; Portland, Maine.

Hayden, Lewis (1815?–1889), Masonic essayist. Born a slave of Presbyterian minister in Kentucky; escaped in 1844 with wife and son through Underground Railroad; settled in Boston, 1849–50; prominent member, Committee of Vigilance to resist Fugitive Slave Act of 1850; his house on Beacon Hill chief Boston "station" of Underground Railroad; recruiting agent for Massachusetts colored regiments in Civil War; had clothing store, was messenger in office of Mass. Secretary of State; elected to legislature, 1873; for years Grand Master, Prince Hall Lodge of black Masons, Boston.

Holley, Joseph Winthrop (1874–1958), autobiographer. Educated at Phillips Academy, Andover, Mass.

James, Thomas (1804–1891), autobiographer. Born a slave in New York State, escaped to Canada in 1821; was minister for time in Massachusetts.

Jeter, Henry Norval (1851–1938), memoirist. After slavery in Virginia, was pastor of Shiloh Baptist Church, Newport, R.I., 1875–1900.

Johnson, Helene (b. 1907), poet. Born in Boston, educated in public schools and at Boston Univ.

Jones, Rhett S. (b. 1940), historian. M.A., Univ. of Connecticut, 1964; M.A., 1972, Ph.D., 1976, Brown Univ.; Assoc. Prof. of History and Afro-American Studies, Brown Univ.

Jordan, Barbara (b. 1936), memoirist. LL.B., Boston Univ. Law School, 1959.

Latimer, Lewis Howard (1848–1928), poet. Born in Chelsea, Mass.; educated in public schools until fifteen, when enlisted in Union Navy; learned mechanical drawing in office of Crosby and Gould, Boston.

Lomax, Pearl Cleage (b. 1948), poet, playwright. Born in Springfield, Mass.

Margetson, George Reginald (b. 1877), poet. Came to United States from native St. Kitts, British West Indies, 1877; was sanitary engineer, Cambridge, Mass.

McClellan, Hassell (b. 1945), essayist. D.B.A., 1978, Asst. Prof. of Management, 1976–80, Harvard Business School; management consultant, Cambridge, Mass., 1980–84; Asst. Prof. of Management, Boston College, 1984––.

McDowell, Deborah (b. 1951), critic, essayist. Asst. Prof. of English, 1979–84, Assoc. Prof., 1984––, Colby College, Maine.

Mitchell, J. Marcus (b. 1921), historian, essayist. Diploma, Feener Technical Institute, Boston, 1952; engineering draftsman, 1950–60; Co-Founder, Boston Afro-American Artists Association, 1962––; Curator, 1965–73, Consulting Curator, 1973––, Museum of Afro-American History; Administrative Assistant for Public Relations, Metropolitan Council for Educational Opportunity, 1973––.

Mix, Mrs. Edward (1832–1884), memoirist. Lived in Connecticut.

Parker, Allen (b. 1837?), author of slave narrative. After escape from slavery in North Carolina, was laborer in New Haven, Conn., and Worcester, Mass.

Plato, Ann, essayist, poet. Lived in Hartford, Conn., where member of Colored Congregational Church, 1841, when James W. C. Pennington the pastor.

Poussaint, Alvin F. (b. 1934), essayist. Asst. Prof. of Psychiatry, Tufts Univ. Medical School, 1967–69; Assoc. Prof. of Psychiatry, Harvard Medical School, 1969––.

Prince, Nancy Gardner (b. 1799), autobiographer. Born in Newburyport, Mass., of African and Indian blood; worked as domestic in Salem and other towns from thirteen to marriage at twenty-five.

Pryor, Robert R. (b. 1927), autobiographer. Was professional boxer in Springfield, Mass.

Randolph, Peter (1825?–1897), autobiographer. Born a slave in Virginia; went with wife and children, along with sixty-three other manumitted slaves, to Boston in 1847; party met at Long Wharf by prominent abolitionists, including William Lloyd Garrison and Wendell Phillips; active in antislavery meetings; worked as laborer, servant, newspaper businessman; studied law, was justice of peace; Baptist minister in Connecticut and Massachusetts; after Civil War, pastor, Ebenezer Baptist Church, Boston, for many years.

Ransom, Reverdy Cassius (1861–1959), memoirist, editor, essayist. Minister, Charles Street A.M.E. Church, Boston, 1905–1907.

Ray, Charles B. (1807–1886), antislavery editor. Born in Falmouth, Mass.; attended Wesleyan Seminary, Wilbraham, Mass., and, until student protests forced him to leave in 1832, Wesleyan Univ., Conn.

Ray, Henrietta Cordelia (1850–1916), poet. Born in Falmouth, Mass., daughter of abolitionist editor and minister, Charles B. Ray.

Remond, Charles Lenox (1810–1873), abolitionist speaker, letter writer. Born and educated in Salem, Mass.; first black lecturer for Massachusetts Anti-Slavery Society, 1838; speaker for years throughout New England; recruiting agent for 54th Mass. Regiment, black, in Civil War; Boston street light inspector, 1865–71; clerk, Boston Custom House, 1871–73; lived in Wakefield, Mass., 1866–73.

Richardson, Ben Albert (b. 1914), biographer. S.T.B., Harvard Univ., 1939.

Roberts, James Deotis, Sr. (b. 1927), essayist, historian. B.D., 1951, S.T.M., 1952, Hartford, Conn., Seminary; Asst. Pastor, Union Baptist Church, Hartford, 1950–52; Minister to Migrants, Conn., summer, 1951–52.

Robinson, Lewis Green (b. 1929), autobiographer. Had various jobs in Boston; attended Calvin Coolidge College, Boston.

Ruggles, David (1810–1849), antislavery editor. Born and lived in Connecticut, 1810–27; operated water-cure establishment in Northampton, Mass., 1842–49.

Rushin, Kate (b. 1951), poet. Fellow, Massachusetts Artists Foundation, 1978; community-based poetry workshop leader, Cambridge; Artist-in-Residence, Boston and area public schools, 1980––.

Rushing, Andrea Benton (b. 1941), essayist, critic. M.A., Simmons College, Boston, 1970; Ph.D., Univ. of Massachusetts, Amherst, 1983; Lecturer in Afro-American Studies, Harvard Univ., 1970–75; Asst. Prof. of Black Studies and English, 1975–80, Assoc. Prof., 1980––, Chair of Black Studies Dept., 1981––, Amherst College.

Russwurm, John B. (1799–1851), antislavery journalist, editor. Born a slave in Jamaica of slave mother and white American father; moved with father to Portland, Maine, then part of Massachusetts, 1812; attended Hebron Academy, 1819–24; B.A., Bowdoin College, 1826; taught in school for black children on lower floor of African Meeting House, Smith Court, Boston.

Sampson, John Patterson (b. 1837), playwright, speaker. Graduate, Comer's College, Boston, 1856; Presiding Elder, New England Conference, African Methodist Episcopal Church, nine years; pastor, Pittsfield, Mass., 1910–11, North Adams, 1911–12.

Senna, Carl (b. 1944), poet, editor. B.A., Boston Univ., 1964.

Simpkins, Thomas V. (b. 1898), poet. Born in Woburn, Mass.

Singleton, George A. (1896–1970), autobiographer. Attended Boston Univ. and Harvard Univ.; African Methodist Episcopal minister in Massachusetts.

Smith, David (b. 1784), autobiographer. Former slave in Maryland, was African Methodist Episcopal minister in Massachusetts.

Sowell, Thomas (b. 1930), memoirist, essayist. B.A., Harvard Univ., 1958; Assoc. Prof. of Economics, Brandeis Univ., 1969–70.

Steptoe, John Lewis (b. 1950), writer-illustrator of children's books. Lived and worked in Peterborough, N.H.

Still, James T., essayist. Physician in Boston, late 19th century.

Stingley, Darryl F. (b. 1951), memoirist. Was professional football player with New England Patriots, 1973–78, until injured and paralyzed; Executive Director, Player Personnel, New England Patriots.

Taylor, Marshall William "Major" (1878–1937), autobiographer, poet. Former professional bicycle racer, settled in Worcester, Mass.

Thomas, Will (b. 1905), fiction writer. Resident of Vermont village after 1946.

Veney, Bethany (b. 1815), author of slave narrative. A slave in Virginia, purchased by Northerner; lived in Providence, R.I., and Worcester, Mass.

Washington, Vivian Edwards (b. 1914), autobiographer. Spent childhood and adolescence in Claremont, N.H.

Weaver, Robert C. (b. 1907), economist essayist. B.S., 1929, M.A., 1931, Ph.D., 1934, Harvard Univ.

Whitfield, James M. (1822–1871), poet. Born in New Hampshire, possibly Exeter.

Wilkens, Lenny (b. 1937), memoirist. Played basketball at Providence College, R.I.; B.A., 1960.

Williams, James H. (1864–1927), autobiographer. Left Fall River, Mass., home at twelve to become sailor.

Worthy, William (b. 1921), journalist. Born in Boston; B.A., Bates College, 1942; was Prof. of Journalism and Afro-American Studies, Boston Univ.

Edward Clark is Professor of English at Suffolk University.